HAUNTED LEADVILLE

HAUNTED LEADVILLE

ERIN TAYLOR

Haunted America

Published by Haunted America
A division of The History Press
An imprint of Arcadia Publishing
Charleston, SC
www.historypress.com

The Pastime Bar and Pioneer on State Street. *Author's collection.*
A group of miners, circa 1880–1900. *Denver Public Library.*

First published 2025

Manufactured in the United States

ISBN 9781467159951

Library of Congress Control Number: 2025940396

CONTENTS

Preface

Ghosts have been around for centuries, passing through different backgrounds and cultures with their individual stories and tales. Some stories are for entertainment, some for warning. Some tales might be rooted in experiences people acquired or an exaggeration to make the lore more persuasive. What are ghosts, after all? They're said to be spirits of the once-living. Of course, they might also have some elemental sides to them, like a water spirits, or something more otherworldly, like aliens from outer space. Some religions teach about angels and demons, while culture may shape how we perceive these supernatural phenomena. Nevertheless, the theme of ghosts and spirits has flowed through the veins of various backgrounds.

The Society of Psychical Research, formed in England in 1882, was a pioneering group of scientists who sought to understand strange and bizarre occurrences. Their work laid the foundation for modern paranormal investigation, and their legacy inspires researchers today. The society's ongoing efforts to collect and analyze data have significantly advanced our understanding of the paranormal.

A 1900 article from *The Herald Democrat* broke down the variations of spirits. "Many spirits are peculiarly luminous. Blue lights have been seen after dark along the country haunts of a daylight ghost of black hue. Many are vaporous and intangible. Others can be distinctively felt. Some are heavy enough that they can weigh their victims down. Others are so filmy that objects can pass through them." The article explains how some spirits appear in pillars or lights, mist formations, and various sensations. This is just one newspaper's opinion, but there are several congruencies about how spirits have been thought to exist over time.

Paranormal investigators explore claims of activity, using scientific equipment to confirm or debunk certain activities. Television and streaming shows may lead us to believe spirits are evil and vindictive. The strange and unknown are displayed as if they should be feared, especially when something happens outside reasonable explanation. An object abruptly moves from unseen hands. A shadow darts across the hall, witnessed by only one person's naked eye. A voice caught on a recorder whispers an inaudible phrase, immediately considered a threat. Not everything on those shows is real or poses a threat.

However, what if we shift our perspective? What if we listen to those inaudible phrases and pay attention to the objects that move? Perhaps these are their attempts to communicate, to say "hello" or to share their stories. What if we were to listen and hear what they have to say?

This personal connection is one of the reasons why I am drawn to the paranormal. Venturing into the darkness to communicate with invisible entities—if they are willing to communicate with me—is a profound experience. My journey into the paranormal began in 2012, and I have discovered that paranormal investigation is much more than sitting in a dark room and asking random questions.

The history of these locations may explain why haunting occurs, such as love, tragedy or trauma. Does the spirit have unfinished business, or is it stuck in an endless loop of residual activity? What makes a haunted location…haunted?

During the summer of 2024, I embarked on a thrilling journey to Leadville, Colorado, to unravel the legend of Elizabeth "Baby Doe" Tabor and the Matchless Mine. Despite growing up in Colorado, I had never ventured to the Cloud City or Magic City, two of the nicknames for the ten-thousand-foot-high city. The enigmatic Baby Doe captivated me, and I was determined to weave her story into my book *Strange Colorado*, which delves into the urban legends of this great state. My books (volumes 1 and 2) were personal explorations of haunted locations, in which I sought paranormal experiences while uncovering the history behind the legends.

I knew little of the Baby Doe legend, except that she was a riches-to-rags woman died in a cabin. Of course, there was so much more to this epic woman. I visited Central City, Colorado, two months before my Leadville stay. This was where Elizabeth lived with her first husband before she

The Presbyterian church "Old Church" on Harrison Avenue, dedicated in 1889. *Author's collection.*

divorced him and moved on to the next mining camp. The Teller House was once a busy hotel, and she lived there momentarily. Several personal items are still there today, a testament to her previous affluent life. Many of these items had to be sold off to pay her debts after the Silver Panic hit the economy in 1893.

My husband, Mike, and I traveled to Leadville and reserved a room at the reportedly haunted Delaware Hotel. Haunted was correct. The beeping started when I set up an electromagnetic frequency (EMF) detector our room, indicating we were not alone in 203. The device is meant to sense energy that is not otherwise explained by a standard power source. My husband slept on as our motion sensor reader indicated that movement was picked up at the foot of our bed. I would later discover that this room was known for its resident ghost. The experience was both thrilling and unnerving, making me realize the depth of the paranormal world.

The next day, we traveled up Seventh Street to the Matchless Mine. Again, I was here as a participant on a tour. The guide knew nothing about our purpose for the visit. When we walked inside the small cabin, history took over. The room was set up to appear as it had in 1935, plus a few displays. There was sadness lingering in the room, and I am not one to claim any psychic ability. Almost in response to my unspoken observation, our

Left: The Delaware Hotel as it stands today. *Author's collection.*

Opposite: The gravesite of Horace and Elizabeth Tabor in Mount Olivet Cemetery in Westminster, Colorado. *Author's collection.*

guide admitted that Mrs. Tabor's spirit was very active in her cabin. My ears perked up. *She is still here?*

The more I researched Leadville, the more I compared it to an onion. Peeling back layers, I discovered that Leadville had so many stories. I was introduced to the work of a local historian, Roger Pretti, who had spent a large amount of time and energy researching the city he called home. Roger authored two books on the history and mysteries of Leadville, along with countless articles. He dove deep into the spookier side of town. I wanted to note that his second book, *Lost Between Heaven and Leadville*, is currently out of print, so I was sadly unable to read what I understand is a thrilling compilation of ghost stories. If you ever get the chance to grab a copy, please do so!

Decked out in Victorian garb, Roger led visitors throughout the cemetery and the historic district through the Leadville by Lamplight Tours (find on Instagram @leadville_by_lamplight_tours). Stories of past residents and

the darker and spookier side of the old mining camp are brought back to life on this walking tour. After Roger passed away, his daughter Rhone continued the legacy of leading these historically accurate tours. Look and book the tour when you visit Leadville to check out these places; you will not be disappointed.

Dear reader, you will notice that Roger's research, along with other reputable sources, such as Edward Blair, influence most of my writing. Of course, some of the sources, such as newspaper articles, may be unverifiable or contradictory, but you can find sources cited in the back of the book for closer examination. Ghost stories started early in Leadville, and the local newspapers quickly captured these alluring tales. Those are shared within these pages. Some of these ghosts have since disappeared, but not all of them have. Walk anywhere in Leadville; you will likely walk past several spirits…and have no idea you did. A cool breeze suddenly on a hot day, a sudden knock or something moving that you swear you did not bump. Perhaps it is an old building. Perhaps you are not alone. Perhaps…would you visit and find out for yourself? Maybe you already live in the area and want to learn more about the history of your beloved town. Leadville is not to be missed. I am ashamed it took me forty years to find it for myself.

Spirits are not to be feared, only understood and listened to. Sit back and relax or cuddle up with a blanket and a light on (or off if you are brave), and read about the histories and mysteries of Leadville, Colorado.

ACKNOWLEDGEMENTS

A very special thank-you goes out to all those who helped me on this spooky journey. Thank you to my husband, Mike, and daughter, Ella, for humoring my trips and extensive dives down research bunny holes. To Richard, for encouraging me to write about Leadville and its hauntings. To Jessica and Alicia, who took a random drive with me to spend a day in a mountain cemetery to help me gather stories. To Yasmine, Rhone, Sherry and Shane, who provided me with valuable stories and experiences. And finally, to a man I'll never get the chance to meet but whose passion will always inspire me: Roger Pretti.

To Leadville and its residents, past and present, without you, none of this book would be possible.

1

LEADVILLE

A BRIEF HISTORY

Before Leadville was a city and Colorado was officially a state, many men set up camps in the Rocky Mountains to search for gold. When ore was discovered in the local area, a community of anyone wanting to strike it rich was developed. Silver made men overnight millionaires who then built Leadville as a testament to their wealth. Some men won, some lost. Let us begin with a bit of history.

In April 1860, miners searched for gold—any sign of flecks—in a seven-mile gulch outside of present-day Buena Vista. Indicating he was about to be rich, Abe Lee shouted, "I've got California in this here pan!" The gully was named California Gulch, but it is unknown if it received the name via Lee's comment or was named after the many California miners passed through the area.

As word got out about the gold placer deposits, many flocked to the area; by the summer of 1860, there may have been up to five thousand new residents along California Gulch. A mining district was established with miner law. Claims were to be located one hundred feet from each other along the gully; if someone abandoned their claim, it was up for anyone to take. It was a revolving door of men, as some were contracted to work only one day a week, and many wanted to stay where they had the chance of obtaining wealth.

The community was named Oro City. The main street was the social hub, covered with cabins, wagons and saloons. Gambling and watching races were pastimes in Oro City, and saloon girls entertained in the bars.

The camp was largely populated with the male demographic, and women were scarce. Most carried rifles and shotguns in case there was a conflict, especially over claims, gambling or women.

The first post office there was established on February 16, 1861, a year after settlement and twelve days before Colorado became a territory. Previously, the closest post office was located in Fairplay, on the other side of the mountain range. Mail was delivered by Pony Duncan, who was hired to travel over the Mosquito Range to gather the parcels from Tarryall, a now-isolated ghost town thirty miles away.

Two months later, on April 12, 1861, the Civil War's first shots occurred in Charleston, South Carolina. The Colorado Territory was a Union sympathizer, and many offered to fight. Nearly two thousand men in the California Gulch were ready but never called. Often, fights broke out across camps, as there were Southerners there, but these scrapes never escalated past heavy words.

Men kept the mines operating, and in 1868, the Printer Boy Mine seduced many miners up the gulch to promises of riches. Oro City was separated into Upper and Lower Oro but had a steady population. Soon-to-be millionaire Horace A.W. Tabor moved to Oro City with his wife, Augusta, and child, Maxcy, from Buckskin, a now–ghost town outside of Fairplay. He had been postmaster and store owner in Buckskin, while his wife managed the post office and successful store, while he scoured the mines for wealth. When the family moved to Oro City, they brought the store with them, and again, Augusta tended to business while Horace was underground.

In 1875, the Arkansas River slowly saw the rise of a small settlement a half mile south of Lower Oro. Malta was, by all means, the beginning of what we know as Leadville. William Stevens and Alvinus Wood surveyed the area for gold placers. They were optimistic they would not leave disappointed but realized they needed water to flush the remaining gold in the gulch. A ditch was built at Rock Hill but was slowed down by a heavy black sludge. An assayer examined the mess, noting that the bothersome material was partially made up of lead carbonates and silver. Stevens and Wood kept the results a secret, finding more lodes in the hills of the impressive ore. Soon, they began collecting abandoned mines or buying those of miners who had given up on the gold. At the end of the year, most of the gulch was owned by these two prospectors.

As the gold seemed to run out, many workers left. Stevens and Wood sent a request out for workers, which about one hundred men from Detroit answered. Conditions were terrible when they arrived in snowy Colorado

Looking at the east side of Harrison Avenue, circa 1877–79. *Photo by George D Wakely.*

Springs, coming up the mountain to a poor working environment. According to author Edward Blair, Stevens had retracted his initial offer of two dollars a day, and instead offered "'dig at thirty cents per cubic yard or build rail fence at twenty-five cents per rod." The men became threatening and demanded funds to be sent back to Michigan; if not, they would take Stevens to the gallows. Terrified, the men ran to Tabor's store. Maxcy Tabor, a teenager who ran the store, was worried the angry men would bust down the door, so he allowed them inside. According to a master's thesis by Marshall Conant Graff, Al Lee was sent to a nearby town, Fairplay, to obtain the funds, while the mob kept an eye on the store. Once completed, most of the mob returned to Detroit.

Within the following year, three Irish brothers came to Oro City to pursue wealth. Rumor has it the Gallagher brothers were directed to Stevens for a mining prospect, and he pointed the trio to a spot away from his claims. Despite this allegedly being a ploy to get the brothers out of the way, the brothers' efforts paid off. Over time, the brothers staked five mining claims before they struck it rich with a silver paycheck. Silver was in abundance, and more would come.

By 1877, Nelson Hallock and Captain Albert Cooper had opened the Carbonate Mine, which made them significant money over the next few years. Other mines opened in the surrounding areas, including Morningstar. The territory's last governor, John L. Rouitt, toured the Morningstar and purchased it for $10,000 before the day ended; it was an investment he worried he would not recover from. After stepping down, he spent all his time working in the mine. However, it paid out; in 1879, ore was discovered in the Morningstar.

As for the town itself, Charles Mater, or as he was known then, "Charley," set up the first shop in Leadville in a log cabin on what would become Chestnut Street. Then Tabor brought his shop directly across from Mater's, bringing the competition. Soon after, the first saloon was built by William "Billy" Nye, and the City Hotel housed up to eight men. Edwin Harrison traveled into town with the St. Louis Smelting and Refining Company and set up a smelter shop on the corner of Chestnut Street and a new road that would later be named after him. Wanting more travelers, Harrison was responsible for building roads to California Gulch.

On September 29, 1877, suffragette Susan B. Anthony stopped at William Nye's saloon to speak on her Colorado tour. The saloon was the largest space to host her, and it is said that the owner hid the bar's alcohol bottles with calico to support her temperance. Allegedly, the men were the roughest she had encountered on her tour, yet the group held respect and courtesy. National Public Radio said in 2018, "Against every expectation, she was warmly applauded, and when she asked for donations, the men passed a hat around and filled it up with gold dust and nuggets." In her diary, Susan wrote, "Spoke in Wm Nyes Saloon—packed with standing men—made a good speech—but alas…might as well have water on a ducks back—as to present arguments to such." She also noted that she could not find a place to stay in the city, a testament to the number of people there. Susan claimed that the twenty-four mining camps in Colorado were challenging to campaign in, so it was a low blow when Colorado voted against women's suffrage the following month. (Colorado would be the first state to enact women's rights in 1893, sixteen years after the suffragette visited the rough and tough mining camp.)

As the city grew, some recognized the need for laws and rules. A meeting was held at Gilbert's wagon, with approximately eighteen in attendance. Their first agenda was naming the city. Tabor insisted on the name Slabtown. Others suggested Carbonate, Cerrusate, Meyer, Leadville and Lead City.

A saloon and gambling hall circa 1880–1910. *Denver Public Library.*

According to the *Leadville Daily/Evening Chronicle* (1879), Leadville was named due to the "lead that is inadvertently carried away by persons who go there and get saucy. A person was buried not long since in the local cemetery who was so full of lead that the bearers thought it was a case of premature putrification."

The governor deemed Leadville an official city, with Horace Tabor as its mayor. His shop at Harrison and Chestnut Streets was deemed the semi-official first bank, as he had the town's only safe. The Lake County Bank became the first official bank in 1878. At 10,430 feet, Leadville became the highest incorporated city in the United States in January 1878, despite recent millionaire Tabor favoring the nickname Slabtown. The California Gulch was filling again with prospectors hungry for the precious ores in the hills. How-to guides were abundant for those traveling to assist them with adjusting to a mountainous or high-altitude climate and to teach them how to make it rich. Steps included finding good-looking land to stake a claim based on advice from an old-timer. Some of the advice was merely suggested by non-miners, who had no idea how to live in a high-altitude climate.

Bird's-eye-view map of Leadville circa 1882. *Denver Public Library.*

The town boomed in 1879, with an approximate twenty thousand residents in Leadville. Newcomers noticed a lack of trees as buildings popped up all over Harrison Avenue and side streets. Lodging, such as rooms in the hotel or boardinghouses, was often tricky to find. In these rooms, a boarder might find a straw mattress and minimal blankets for fear they might be stolen. One lodger rented out blankets to avoid theft. Housing was scarce or expensive, but some could afford to build a cabin. Those who did not have housing may have pop-up tents throughout the streets. "Many, probably hundreds, had to sleep where they could find a spot, be that a barn, on the street, under a doorstep, or even an empty barrel," according to Leadville historian and author Roger Pretti.

Henry Gaw moved out to Leadville from Idaho Springs with his family and broke ground for the town's first brewery in 1878. By 1880, Columbine Beer was being manufactured and shipped all over the state. For those who did not care for the hops, Isaac Hougland made soda water to sell, while a more extensive soda shop, managed by Frank Schmidt and F.M. Aldinger, was located on Chestnut Street. Groceries and restaurants were expensive, with prices dependent on availability. Fresh dairy products were a rarity in the area.

Education was important, and students were taught in cabins. When a larger institution was necessary, money was put forth to develop the Central School on Spruce Street. By the end of 1881, around 1,200 students were enrolled.

Nevertheless, Leadville was the place to be, and people came from all over. Some notable travelers ventured through the town, including outlaw Jesse James and famed Tombstone shooter John "Doc" Holliday. Irish poet and playwright Oscar Wilde came through Leadville in April 1882 to speak at the Tabor Opera House during his only U.S. tour. His audience consisted of working men, and Wilde chose to read from the autobiography of Benvenuto Cellini. Someone inquired why Cellini was not reading it, to which Wilde responded that he was dead. Immediately, a voice piped up, "Who shot him?" Wilde later expressed that he felt the miners of Leadville were "ready but not rough. They were polished and refined compared with the people I met in larger cities further East. The revolver is their book of etiquette. It teaches lessons that are not forgotten."

Horace Tabor invited Wilde and his manager to visit the successful Matchless Mine. The poet ungracefully rode a "rickety bucket" down the shaft to enjoy dinner at the mine, which he described: "Having got into the heart of the mountain, I had supper, the first course being whisky, the second whisky and the third whisky." He would later reflect in his writings his amusement at the "only rational method of art criticism," as he stopped at one saloon where there was a sign not to shoot the pianist who was "doing his best."

Leadville High School was located on Spruce Street circa 1881–85. *Denver Public Library.*

Leadville was even in the running to be the state capitol, with an area of town being designated as "Capitol Hill," the location for the potential government building. But as most already know, the city lost to Denver.

These streets were noisy, dirty and busy day and night. The roughest and toughest spent their time on State Street, home of the brothels, gambling dens and thieves. Locals knew enough to avoid certain areas of town if they valued their lives.

The dusty streets were unkempt. Later, the silver-lined roads needed constant upkeep when the "smelter slag," the waste left over from refining the precious metals, was utilized. If the streets were not bad enough, the sidewalks could injure someone. The more someone walked the street or walkway, the more they learned to deviate from the ruffage.

Deaths were commonly attributed to "climate, diet, housing, hard work, and hard liquor…and doctors," according to Edward Blair. In 1881, sixty-one physicians and surgeons were listed. However, only twenty-three were graduates of known medical schools. Some of the city's deaths may have been caused indirectly by poor care. A dozen dentists were also on the scene in 1880; one, Henry Rose, set up shop under a streetlight at Chestnut and Harrison Streets. His family legacy stuck around Leadville for almost seventy-five years.

The population of Leadville was diverse, with half being white Americans. The Irish settlers were the next largest group, living on Fifth, Sixth and Seventh

One of the busy Leadville roads circa 1880–85. *Denver Public Library.*

Streets, but some resided on Chicken Hill with the Swedish immigrants. The Germans made Leadville home, bringing beer gardens and pastries to the city. Not to be ignored, the English, Cornish and Canadians were known to bring hard work to the camps. Enslaved people fleeing from the South made a camp on South State Street, which became known as Coon Row (a reference to a racial slur for Black people). Black people were welcomed to the town without restrictions and could live among other settlers; however, they had separate churches and schools. Fraternal organizations, such as the Masons, Odd Fellows and the Elks, were designated from the early camp days. Most races were welcome in town, and no one was more special than the other. However, there were two exceptions. Anyone from an Asian background was banned, as miners were convinced they were bad news for the economy. The same went for the neighboring Ute Natives, as there was an old philosophy that they were better off dead.

Leadville was a male-dominated community where women who needed income found themselves in various professions—not always the most esteemed. Some of the girls in town were as young as twelve—orphans, husband-hunters or girls hiding from unhappy homes. Edward Blair described, "All seemed to be running; some after something, others from something." The town's high-standing ladies were involved with millinery and dressmaking. The Irish women oversaw the laundry market, while women owned 25 percent of the town's boardinghouses. Then there were

Leadville looking north, circa 1885. *Photo by Alfred Brisbois.*

A view of the Iron Silver Mine around 1882–1900. *Photo by William Henry Jackson.*

those who worked in the dance halls, saloon waitresses and the women who worked the red-light district.

Everyone in the area had one goal: to be prosperous. Many did strike it rich, and many died poor. Those who died found a bed in the local cemetery. Murders, overdoses and mining deaths were common endings. The Sherman Silver Act, which ruled that the government was required to buy 4.5 million ounces of silver each month, was enacted in 1890. This lasted three years before the crash. The new president at the time, Grover Cleveland, was against bimetallism, which may have led to the financial crisis. The Sherman Silver Purchase Act was repealed by Congress, with the domino effect causing the Panic of 1893. The price of silver decreased to sixty-two cents per ounce, and many found themselves without work. Needing to make ends meet, numerous people left the city, while others took up odd jobs or a life of crime.

Even after the Silver Panic of 1893 struck the town, the mines continued to run in the area. Those who did not leave to find other income stayed in the Cloud City. By 1895, the population had dwindled to fifteen thousand. An iced structure was built as a castle to draw in customers and tourists, complete with an ice rink and two ballrooms. The Crystal Carnival was held in the spacious Ice Palace from January 1 to March 28, 1896, as spring drew near. Between the financial costs of construction and employment and the strangely warm winter weather that caused the ice to melt, the Ice Palace did not earn the economic boost Leadville had hoped for. This was the first and only Ice Palace in Leadville.

That summer, the miners grew weary of their working conditions and pay. The catalyst for the 1896 miners' strike in Leadville was the desire for higher pay. Workers were making $2.50 and struggling with the price of living. The Cloud City Miners' Union's requests to increase pay to a baseline of $3 per day were dismissed. On June 20, across 13 mines, 968 men walked out in protest. This resulted in mine closures, impacting production and causing the unemployment of 2,300 men by June 23. Mine owners gave the strikers until August 22 to return to work, but most of them ignored this. Now, the owners looked elsewhere for assistance.

The angry men advanced when they learned that two mines were operating on the side with lower-paid employees. After midnight on September 21, hundreds of men approached the Coronado Mine and engaged in a shootout, complete with explosives. Unscathed, the strikers fled after an oil tank burst into flames, the fire stretching to houses on East Eighth Street. The nearby

The Ice Palace in 1896. *Denver Public Library.*

Maid of Erin Mine was almost destroyed by fire but quickly extinguished. Not done with the night, the remaining rioters crossed a mile to the Robert Emmet Mine, where they engaged in the same destructive behavior. One night's actions resulted in five men's deaths, along with at least thousands of dollars' worth of damage between the three mines. Concerned about further violence, Governor McIntire sent the militia to maintain control and allow the mines to continue operation. On average, over four hundred militiamen were in camp at any given time. For lodging, the Ice Palace structure was dismantled so that the material could be used for barracks.

Tensions remained high, mainly when the state supported the mine owners. Strikers either left town or returned to the mines; others resorted to violence and aggression. With no change in wages, the strikers lost hope and returned to work for their old pay. After nine long months, the strike ended on March 9, 1897.

By 1900, the city had two banks, several places of worship, a new high school and over one hundred saloons. The remaining mines continued their operations. Sulfides were discovered in the mines from 1905 to 1910, and they vitalized the economy. Then the town flourished again when zinc was discovered to be profitable in 1911. Previously, the zinc mineral had been dismissed. Zinc mills flourished through the Leadville mountainsides, as the mineral was used to coat steel for rust aversion. This protected weapons and vehicles in wartime, while, in World War II, zinc was used as an alternative to making pennies, as copper was being diverted for ammunition. Leadville flourished.

It is also noted that during World War II, Camp Hale was established as a temporary training facility in Pando Valley, approximately fifteen miles from Leadville; from 1942 to 1945, soldiers trained for rough winter conditions at high altitudes and were taught to use skis and snowshoes. Morale was low, and the camp was nicknamed "Camp Hell." After 1945, the camp was used as a winter warfare facility for Fort Carson soldiers out of Colorado Springs, and from 1959 to 1964, the camp was used by the Central Intelligence Agency to train Tibetan soldiers covertly. Permanently closed in 1965, the location was placed in the National Register of Historic Places in 1992 and maintained by the United States Forest Service. Visitors can stop by today and see the reminders of the old camp. As for the local ski resorts, most were founded by Camp Hale soldiers who enjoyed the activity and wanted to continue after the war ended.

Today, Leadville is a popular stop for history lovers, outdoor enthusiasts and college students. Colorado Mountain College was established in 1965,

The Masonic building on Harrison Avenue. *Author's collection.*

and many students enjoy their education and immediate access to the vast outdoors. Since several ski resorts are nearby, getting to the slopes quickly is easy. During the warmer months, the lakes are full of fish, many hiking trails seduce those who want to explore in the clouds and there are often marathons and bicycle races.

Then there are the spirits of old Leadville. From the dawn of the town to the present, the hauntings of Leadville remind us of the history and lore of the great mining town. Take a walk down any historic road; a spirit or two is bound to keep an eye on you. Settle in, take a bucket down the shaft or grab a donkey as we venture into haunted Leadville.

2
Mining District Hauntings

By the time Leadville became officially incorporated in 1878, silver mines were popping up throughout the town's surrounding gulches. Men like Horace Tabor became millionaires overnight. Within a few years, the population had almost doubled, as miners traveled in droves to the town to stake a claim. Many mines were built and equipped with different designs—and not always the safest fashions. Tensions were heightened in the hills. Many died in these mines as a result of accidents, and many also died because of conflict. Of course, the dead men here do sometimes tell tales. While not every mine had an otherworldly visitor, the following are just a few ghost tales of the mining district.

Nearing the fall of 1876, three Irish brothers traveled into the Oro City camp looking for advice. The naive newcomers were directed to Iron Hill, where Billy Stevens dismissively told the greenhorns to go over the hill and dig under a tree. The brothers, John, Patrick and Charles, followed the so-called advice, despite the realization that the man was yanking their chain. Their first shaft was constructed on the east side of Iron Hill. Edward Blair said this was no easy feat, as man and animal power were utilized to work the shaft—there was nothing of the machinery of modern times. The Gallagher brothers' hard work paid off. They staked more claims in the area over the winter before finding what they wanted: riches. Silver was discovered, along with zinc and a small amount of gold!

The summer of 1877 saw the discovery of the Carbonate Mine (which named the hill on which it stood) by Nelson Hallock and Captain Albert

Cooper. The mine produced thousands of dollars' worth of ore within the year, making the men successful. Hallock was instrumental in the early development of Leadville and eventually moved to Denver, where he became the president of the Colorado Iron Works. Captain Cooper stayed longer than his counterpart before eventually returning to the sea, which started his career years prior.

Mining in Leadville took off with the declaration of silver in the hills. Men like James Joseph "J.J." Brown worked the mines to hit the pay load. After getting married in 1886, the Browns lived above the mining district in a camp named Stumptown (some sources write it as "Stumpftown") before moving to Leadville's West Seventh Street in 1889. His success was found in the Little Johnny Mine, which produced silver and gold. With a new fortune amassed while others were going broke from the 1893 Silver Panic, the Browns moved to a Denver mansion on Pennsylvania Street in 1894 at the request of Brown's wife, Margaret, also known to some as "Maggie." She became well known in international society, despite being snubbed by Denver's affluent circle. While she was busy with charity work, Margaret became most famous for her heroic efforts during the sinking of the luxury passenger-liner ship the *Titanic*. She would forever be known as the legendary "Unsinkable Molly Brown"; the talented Kathy Bates portrayed her in the 1997 award-winning film *Titanic*. She never went by Molly while she was alive; it's a nickname

Looking at Leadville to the north, circa 1877–79. *William Henry Jackson.*

that was given to her after her 1932 death. Some sources have suggested that Margaret later helped Elizabeth "Baby Doe" Tabor during her Matchless Mine days (another haunted story we will explore later).

As mentioned in the previous chapter, Horace Tabor made his millions with the South Pittsburg Mine on Fryer's Hill and then again with the Chrysolite and Matchless Mines in the nearby area. The story with the Chrysolite Mine was that the previous owner tried to dupe him before Tabor purchased the moneymaker! Legend says that "Chicken Bill" Lovell propped ore in the mine to entice Tabor into thinking there was more value. The joke was on Lovell when Tabor's men went down several more feet (anywhere from ten to twenty-five feet) and struck ore.

Mining guidebooks were aplenty, with tips on getting rich quickly in the camp. Of course, the guides varied in information and opinion. Many were about how to live in the camp, including provisional needs like cooking ware and appropriate clothing. However, very few provided instructions on how to work a mine. Men started working in dangerous conditions with minimal training or expertise.

Directions to strike it rich were simple: a miner needed to find a good piece of land and then mark the claim with six upright stakes as the law dictated. Speed was a significant factor in filing the patent claim, and the shaft was expected to be dug in a certain amount of time. As mining proved difficult, mainly depending on the geographical features of the land, three to four men were ideal to provide the shaft build. These men were paid $2.00 to $3.50 a day for their work. With the recommended amount of labor, the shaft hole could be dug at an average of five feet per day. Timbers were

The hoist house at the Matchless Mine. *Photo courtesy of Shane Kinney.*

used as support as the workers descended. As the hole was deepened, miners often used a bucket hoist system to lower equipment. Everything went down the shaft via the bucket, including the burrows.

Claims that bore names such as Breece, Iron and Chicken Hill popped up throughout the hills. Names were chosen carefully. Many mines were named after ladies like Minnie, Little Eva and Tootie Gaylord. Some did not want to acknowledge their gals, choosing unique names like Slim Jim or Black Cloud. By 1890, there were approximately seventy to ninety working mines in Leadville, with many more unsuccessful. The chances of getting rich drew men like moths to a flame, and the odds were likely to burn them.

A tragic incident occurred at the Chrysolite Mine on November 9, 1880, when two men lost their lives at the Little Silver no. 2 shaft on the property. Joseph McCoskey started feeling the effects of poisonous gas down in the bowels of the mine and began gesturing to be pulled up through the hoist system. The gas was too much, and he fell out of the bucket elevator down the shaft, only eighteen inches from the top ground. His foreman tried to save him, but he was not close enough. Another worker, Alexander McHardy, went to retrieve the man's lifeless body when he, too, was overcome by the noxious fumes. Both deceased were brought back to the surface, where they were taken to their respective burial places.

Then there was George S. Robinson, a world traveler from Michigan who found paydirt in several properties. When word got out that his mine, the Smuggler, was to be taken over, he hired men to watch over the property. On Thanksgiving Day 1880, Robinson visited the mine and checked the Smuggler's security. An observant guard heard him walking and shouted to see who was lurking about. Instead of responding, a satisfied Robinson walked away—but not before the guard took a shot through the door. Robinson died from his abdominal wound two days later, but he asked that the guard who shot him not be held liable for only doing his job.

The Moyer Mine also saw its share of loss…and the ghost stories started early. Up on California Gulch once stood a one-hundred-foot shaft that employed about sixty men under the management of William Stevens with the Iron Silver Mining Company. Legend states that there was an unpredictable cave-in that killed twelve miners, and their bodies were never recovered. Also unknown was *when* this was said to have occurred. The spirits of the dead men started visiting the working miners, as Giusippe Lombardi experienced one day. He claimed to see his dead cousin working alongside him; the cousin had left their home country months before and had not been heard from since.

Left: Mining shaft of the Matchless Mine. *Author's collection.*

Below: A map of Leadville mines in 1880. *Author's collection.*

Iron Silver Mine, circa 1882–1900. *Photo by William Henry Jackson.*

Considered congenial, these spirits may not have wanted the living to suffer the same fate that occurred to them. Other fatal accidents resulted from falls and explosives, whereupon these ghosts might be any of those souls. Interestingly, there was European lore of the Welsh Tommyknockers, who were said to be little creatures that protected miners while also causing trouble in the mine. Some believe that the Tommyknockers are the spirits of miners, still protecting the living. Of course, those in Leadville mines would be no different.

In 1899, John Comfrey claimed to have experienced a "spook" in the Moyer Mine. According to *The News Reporter*, the spirit appeared to Comfrey in the mine, to which he reacted by falling down a seventy-foot ladder "while the ghost sat on an ore sack, crossed his legs, and smiled at the doughty miner's precipitation." Luckily, Comfrey suffered only a minimal injury. The newspaper said he hightailed home and did not want to come back. Brave Comfrey came back to work after a few days of rest.

Moyer Mine is also the location of the most popular ghost in the mining district, the Gallagher Ghost. Not of relation to the Irish brothers from Iron Hill, Senator Joseph P. Gallagher met an unfortunate end when he entered the mine to challenge the ghosts. The *Daily Sentinel* recalled one story where a spirit appeared to Gallagher. Supposedly, the spirit warned him of the potential danger, but Gallagher ignored the message. As a result, he fell down a shaft and off this mortal coil. His angry ghost is said to wander the mine now, carrying a pick and crying, "Beware!"

It is a frightful story, but it is not true. Gallagher's untimely death came while he was inspecting explosives in February 1900. According to Roger Pretti, after working in the mine for two weeks, the senator was killed when the "parts of his anatomy were truncated in an explosion in a drift." Nevertheless, his ghost still prevails. Sometimes, the bigger fish story is grander than the truth.

Author's note: Tales of the Gallagher Ghost and the spirit of a lady in black were often used to get children to behave. According to the legend, the woman, dressed in mourning clothes, was forever waiting on Chicken Hill for the miner who would never come to her.

Not to be excluded from the ghost stories was another ghostly woman seen in the New Discovery Mine. The 1879 story was so tantalizing that a newspaper in New York covered it. The ghostly woman was seen by several miners, who "attempted several times to run her up a bucket, but she always slips through their fingers and flying to the end of the drift faces her tormentors and spits fire," according to an article in the *Leadville Daily/Evening Chronicle*. Those who saw her supposedly never came back. Who she was, we may never know. Today, the mine lies under an empty field on Fryer Hill, but legend claims she is waiting, lurking in the abandoned tunnels below.

Speaking of tunnels, the Fortuna Tunnel was the scene of a grisly death. Phillip Nash was the self-proclaimed king of Leadville, but the rumor was that he was not the best of character. An Irishman who came to Colorado for his payout upset the wrong man. On August 23, 1885, Nash tried to enter the Fortuna Tunnel and was stopped by Henry Kirby, whose boss supposedly directed him not to let anyone enter. When Nash did not listen, he was almost decapitated and instantly killed when Henry Kirby attacked him with an axe. One unnamed news source said that Kirby played it cool after the undoing, returning home to change into his best suit. He then lit a cigar before turning himself in to the local officials.

Despite the claim that Nash had previously threatened and called him profane names in the witnesses of others, the court found the killing unjustified and not done in self-defense. The local newspaper covered the case; Kirby was found guilty of the murder, and the judge pronounced his sentencing "'with all the convenient speed to the state penitentiary of the state of Colorado to be…kept and confined therein to hard labor for and during four years, to be fed and clothed as the law directs, and you will pay for the costs of this action.'" One legend, as shared by author Roger Pretti: while Kirby was working on an elevator with two other men, a fourth person was in the cart with them for a moment. The presence pushed Kirby against the elevator door "and uttered a curse" before vanishing from view. This may have been Nash seeking vengeance for his untimely death.

Nash was buried in Evergreen Cemetery, and his epitaph immortalized the phrase "Self-Proclaimed King of Leadville." Of course, his spirit is said to be lurking in the shadows of the tunnel. According to Rhone Pretti, Nash still haunts the Fortuna Tunnel. Is he seeking revenge for losing his head? Or is he trying forever to get into the place where he was permanently stopped? We may never know.

Death came for workers of the Mikado Mine (established in 1885); Roger Pretti documented that by 1891, at least six men had met their untimely deaths in terrible accidents. Stories of the phantoms came quickly and seemed to haunt every level of the mine. Miners were frightened by icy hands, voices and apparitions. Pretti described one encounter: "One employee, confronted by the shade of a miner wearing ragged brown coveralls, an old hat, and blue snow spectacles, ran his shovel through the misty form, which promptly vanished in the lurid candlelight." Some miners thought mimicking ghostly noises, such as moaning and bell ringing, was a hilarious way to frighten newer miners or bosses. It worked, as some hastily left after collecting their last pay. The odd noises continued even after the pranksters were instructed to halt their tomfoolery.

The grave of Phillip Nash in Evergreen Cemetery, the "self-proclaimed king of Leadville." *Author's collection.*

Some spirits appeared among the gulches, where the mines stood waiting. In 1886, Harry Harrington lived in a cottage in Strawberry Gulch on the west side of Leadville. Near his house was the location of three hangings for one murder, one of the executed being Si Meunich (other news sources called him a mixture of "Cyrus" or "Minich"), who declared his innocence until the final drop. Harrington claimed that the spirit of the dead man was haunting his cottage with "uncanny displays" and noises that almost caused the nervous man to flee. Harry insisted others had seen the specter and offered to the "night hawks to drop down and see him at the midnight hour," as written in *The Herald Democrat*. Could it be that Meunich was attempting to prove his innocence from beyond the grave?

Leadville was home to many mines, as many as 1,300 shafts, 155 tunnels and 1,600 prospect holes, which have been confirmed over the years. Many made men wealthy; others left broken or dead men. Of hundreds of mines, only a few remain visible among the hills surrounding Leadville. There might also be hundreds of miles of abandoned mines under the hills, but you would never be able to guess this is the case. Visitors can travel up the Silver Kings route and take in the marvels of the slopes that once held vast shafts and structures, starting at Chicken Hill and ending at Fryer Hill. Will you see a ghost? Who knows, but you will see fragments from a once-booming area, slivers of time haunting the hills and residual memories of the greatest silver mining camp.

3

"Baby Doe" and the Matchless Mine

Leadville was established by men who were pursuing their riches, and founding member Horace Tabor pursued something else that would place him in a scandal. There was much to say about one of the founding men leaving his wife of twenty-four years for a much younger woman. After a lavish affair and marriage, the money soon ran out due to a government act—and so did the extravagant lifestyle. It was a riches-to-rags story that led to one of the biggest legends of Colorado. The following is the so-called illicit tale of Horace and Elizabeth "Baby Doe" Tabor.

Horace Austin Warner Tabor married his first wife, Augusta Pierce, in Maine on January 31, 1857. She was his employer's daughter. The newlyweds moved west and started farming in Kansas. Nathaniel Maxcy was born in November 1857. Two years later, the Tabors left their farm for the gold promises of the Rocky Mountains.

They planted their roots in Buckskin, building Augusta's shop, while Horace acted as postmaster. When he could, Horace searched for gold. After a decade, the family packed up again and moved to the Leadville area to chase the word of potential wealth. Here, they established three shops, which Augusta also managed. Speculation said Horace was a good man with an equally good heart. Once, fresh eggs were unavailable for months. A traveler caught wind of this and, hoping to make a dollar, brought some eggs over Mosquito Pass. Horace purchased the eggs and sold them for the same price that he bought them. When asked why he did not increase the price, Horace said it had been so long since the men had tasted something delicious that he did not want to take advantage.

Above, left: Horace Tabor, circa 1883–90. *Above, right*: Augusta Tabor, circa 1870–80. *Denver Public Library.*

Opposite: Elizabeth "Baby Doe" Tabor, circa 1885–90. *Photo by A.E. Rinehart.*

One day in 1878, two miners came into Horace's shop. They mentioned the ore they had found in the nearby California Gulch, and Tabor jumped at a grubstake (which means he offered supplies as a trade for part of the profit). This was a fortunate turn of events. The Little Pittsburg Mine produced enough to put Tabor on the map as a millionaire. Tabor invested in other profitable Colorado mines, including the nearby Chrysolite and Matchless Mines. He had his house on Harrison Avenue relocated to Fifth Street. Horace appeared to give back to his community, as Leadville was graced with an opera house, a gas company and a telephone company. After moving his family to Denver in 1879, he founded the Tabor Grand Opera House in downtown Denver, declared the grandest theater between St. Louis and San Francisco. Life was going well for the Tabors until a young woman came to Cloud City.

Elizabeth Bonduel McCourt was born in 1854 in Oshkosh, Wisconsin, to middle-class Irish Catholic parents Peter McCourt and Elizabeth Nellis; she was the fifth of fourteen children. The family lived decently on the income from Peter's successful clothing shop. Young Elizabeth was the prettiest child by far; it was apparent to others that she was well taken care of. This also helped find the young lady a husband. William "Harvey" Doe Jr. fell for the maiden after she won an ice skating competition, even though she was said to have cheated. Their wedding on June 22, 1877, was so well attended that not all the guests could fit comfortably in the Catholic church.

Soon after the wedding, Elizabeth followed her new husband and his father to Colorado on her honeymoon. The elder Mr. Doe left the couple in Denver as he traveled up the mountain to check his mining claim in Central City. The couple followed two weeks later.

Here, she incurred the nickname that would haunt her for the rest of her life: the local miners called her "Baby Doe." In the city, Harvey began working in the Fourth of July Mine. Likely because of boredom, Elizabeth joined him in working in the mine. This was unheard of, as married women were supposed to stay in the home. There was also a rumor that she worked at the mine because her husband could not provide for their household on a single income. Eventually, Harvey had a negative shift in behavior, and it was said that he started drinking more and womanizing. There may have been some abuse toward his wife. Other speculations said that their stillborn son did nothing to help strengthen their union. After Harvey was seen entering a bordello, Elizabeth divorced him on the grounds of adultery. Divorce was a rarity in this era. Wanting to stay in Colorado, she traveled toward the town that was said to make men rich. She arrived in Leadville around 1880 to join her friend Jacob Sandelowsky, who had a new shop on Harrison Avenue. If he was a romantic interest, the interest fizzled out. She appeared to have her eyes on another catch.

The leading man of Leadville, Horace, met Elizabeth at the Saddle Rock Café, and soon, gossip spread that there was an affair between the two. Elizabeth was twenty-four years his junior, and it is noted that she was born around three years after Horace and Augusta wed. Their not-so-secret rendezvous started at the Windsor Hotel before he moved her to an elegant suite at the Clarendon Hotel next to the Tabor Opera House. (It is said that the walkway between the buildings was more manageable for the two to sneak around in.) Horace lavished Elizabeth with gifts and was said to have also paid off all the old debt she carried from her first marriage. They were in love, so it was said.

The *Rocky Mountain News* called the new lady the "handsomest woman in Colorado." Elizabeth had a clear complexion, similar to a white lily with a bit of rose blush, a "great wealth of light brown hair…large dreamy blue eyes, that sometimes kindle with enthusiasm," and it was said she "walks as majestically as the queen." Moreover, she lived like a queen.

As their marriage became more estranged, Augusta sued Horace for desertion. Not appearing affected, he replied by filing for divorce in 1882. Their divorce was final in January 1883. After the divorce, Augusta was financially secure, keeping her two stores and her millions. Despite her financial means, she was emotionally distraught over the divorce and threw her energy into the Unitarian Church. Augusta also founded the Pioneer Ladies' Aid Society. Respiratory problems claimed her life while she was living in California in 1895, the day before what would have been her thirty-eighth wedding anniversary. Her body was brought back to Colorado to be interred in Denver's Riverside Cemetery.

Some hot gossip said that Elizabeth and Horace were secretly wed by a justice of the peace in St. Louis on September 30, 1882, prior to his divorce, with her brother Peter as a witness. However, the wedding would not be considered legal, since his divorce had not been finalized. Two months after the ink dried on the divorce papers, Elizabeth and Horace were married in an elaborate ceremony in Washington, D.C. Horace had recently been appointed an interim state senator. Their guests included members of high society, senators, members of Congress, and then-President Chester Arthur. Due to the word of scandal, many of the high society and political First Ladies were not in attendance. The wife of Colorado's ex-Senator Henry Teller tore up the invitation and returned the scraps to Leadville as her response. No expense was too great for the couple, as evidenced by the wedding invitations' silver linings. Meanwhile, precious silver laced her intricate wedding dress. The wedding was a glamorous and grand show, a testament to their riches.

After the wedding, the newlyweds temporarily lived at the Windsor Hotel before they moved into a new Denver mansion, where they lived with the finest things. Horace spoiled his new wife with jewelry estimated to cost between $75,000 and $90,000. One jeweled necklace was rumored to have once been Queen Isabella's—the one she used to finance Christopher Columbus's 1492 excursion across the sea. It did not seem to bother them that most of the society circles snubbed them after the scandal of their affair came out. Mostly, they snubbed Elizabeth.

In 1883, Horace started building the four-story Tabor Grand Hotel in Leadville, complete with dormers and a widow's walk. He continued to try his hands at politics, although he had an unsuccessful run in the lieutenant governor elections. Elizabeth gave birth to two daughters, Elizabeth "Lily" in 1884 and Rose Mary "Silver Dollar" in 1889. A son was stillborn in 1888; Elizabeth would later express in her writings that her two stillborn babies visited her dreams.

Their lavish lifestyle would eventually end. The Silver Panic of 1893 impacted the cost of silver. With no further value from the ore, Horace was losing income fast. Their fine luxuries were sold off to pay debts. The family lived in the mansion, watching their belongings get sold off while sitting without electricity, servants or water. According to author Judy Nolte Temple, Horace and Elizabeth were "pretending to the children that they were 'camping.'" Five years later, Horace became the postmaster of Denver. Still, Elizabeth and the children stayed with him as the pennies dwindled. Many of Horace's old partners dismissed his requests for loans, but Maxcy Tabor did help a slight bit with his inheritance from his mother.

In 1899, Horace died of appendicitis with his wife at his side. Some stories speculate that he said, "Hold onto the Matchless," as money was still to be made. This statement has never been confirmed. His funeral and procession were said to have been attended by thousands of mourners. A band played Chopin's "Funeral March" while the body was moved from the governor's mansion to the grave site. The impressive event left a crowd pushing to get inside the church service. Horace was buried in the Calvery Cemetery in a private ceremony; Elizabeth was said to have fainted during the last rites. An hour after holding silent sorrow, she left the graveside. Two large stones and dirt filled the grave in a final goodbye. As Horace died a legend, Elizabeth was still ostracized as a beautiful widow.

Without a place to live, she packed up the children and what she had left and returned to Leadville. Horace's words played in her mind. Leadville had not forgotten the affair; no open arms were waiting for her. Scraping by, she worked odd jobs to make ends meet. Sheriffs took the Matchless to sale in 1901 as collateral for her incurring debt, but the mine was saved by Elizabeth's sister Claudia McCourt McCabe in 1902. Her sister granted her power of attorney to make all decisions for the mine. Elizabeth and her daughters moved into the abandoned one-room supply shack beside the mine when they had no other options. This was her final home for thirty years, and she never let it go. While she had the opportunity to be remarried, Elizabeth never pursued another marital relationship.

As a teenager, Lily moved to Wisconsin, where she lived with McCourt relatives and cut ties with the Tabor name. Silver Dollar stayed in Leadville for a while before becoming a journalist in Denver. She often interviewed the high-society women who had spoken so poorly of the family in the past. Occasionally, she would try to help her mother. After moving to Chicago to pursue the entertainment industry, Silver Dollar died mysteriously in 1925—said to be the result of a fatal scalding in her living arrangements. When informed of her sister's death, Lily claimed her sister was alive, insisting the deceased woman had a different appearance. "My sister entered a convent against the wishes of the family," Lily informed the press.

Elizabeth was also in denial, believing the story about the convent. While she read the articles about Silver's death after hours in the public library, she dismissed the notion that the dead woman was her daughter. She told an acquaintance, "I'm not going to pay for the burial of an imposter." She never accepted the loss, as she held on to the idea that the Matchless would be passed on to her daughter one day. Silver Dollar was buried in Chicago, as her maternal uncle paid $300 for funerary expenses. The younger daughter of Horace and Elizabeth Tabor went to her eternal rest without any family present.

Over time, people started to talk about Elizabeth's status as a "mad woman." One rumor was that the nearby water was toxic, which may have contributed to her lack of sanity. This theory was squashed when the water was tested and determined to be safe to consume. Those who knew Elizabeth insisted she was not insane or delusional. Even her brother Phillip McCourt later commented on her insight regarding Silver's possible death: "She said, 'Phil, I do not know she is dead. They tell me that she died in a fire in Chicago. However, they were not sure at first. I did not see the body they said was my little girl. How can I be sure she is dead? And if I am not sure of that, I must believe she is alive.' Did that sound like the speech of an insane woman?" An old Leadville resident, Mr. Frank Zaitz, often assisted Elizabeth, and he respected the woman she claimed had better organization than any attorney. "She wasn't crazy but only about one thing—the Matchless. You couldn't talk to her and believe she was crazy."

Nevertheless, Elizabeth was proud of the ways she lived at the cabin. The walls were lined with newspaper, which helped keep the heat from the small stove inside. Once the silver queen, Elizabeth lived in squalor, only with her dreams of the mine restoring its millions.

Elizabeth Tabor during a visit to Denver around 1921–22. *Denver Public Library.*

Perhaps she was never mad, only heartbroken over being gossiped about and jeered at. She occasionally walked the mile into town while wearing gunny sacks on her feet to fulfill her other needs, which included immersing herself in books at the library and praying at the church. When she traveled out of Leadville, Elizabeth ventured to Denver, where people stared at her and pointed her out to their children—like a spectacle on display.

Elizabeth documented what she called visions and dreams she experienced. She was intrigued by "Dreamworld," where she thought to communicate with the dead. With a strong Catholic faith, Elizabeth created writings that were often themed with God and the devil. Some historians have suggested that her writings have underlying emotional impacts, such as the guilt she felt as a parent. Her ramblings were her own, as she wrote to herself, likely never imagining her words would appear elsewhere. Were her visions and dreams nothing more than a diary, a way for her to process these emotions in a world where talk therapy was far from developed?

The mine would never produce more ore; Shorego Mining Company tried after it purchased the mine when it went into foreclosure in the 1920s.

Shorego owner J.K. Mullen was said to back Elizabeth by paying off her mortgage; when he died, his heirs chose not to evict the frail woman. Socialite Margaret "Maggie" Brown was still considerably wealthy after her husband made his fortune in Leadville and was said to support Elizabeth when able. However, Elizabeth often declined help or handouts; it was rare for her to accept charity. When she ventured to town, she often asked merchants to put her items on the Matchless tab, something the store owners knew would never be repaid. A year before her death, Elizabeth was almost moved into a small house, which she resisted, as she needed to keep watch over her mine. It was known around town that she sometimes carried a shotgun and was a good marksman. The *Rocky Mountain News* described Elizabeth as "a part of the legend of Leadville, hardly a part of its life."

On March 7, 1935, Elizabeth's neighbor and friend Sue Bonnie was concerned when she realized she had not seen Elizabeth recently. Sue often visited Elizabeth, who told her life stories while talking to spirits over a Ouija board. On this day, smoke was not seen billowing out of Elizabeth's chimney stack, which was odd, since it was springtime in the Rockies. So, Sue went to investigate. Inside, Elizabeth "Baby Doe" Tabor was found frozen on the floor of her cabin, near her stove, dead from cardiac failure. There was plenty of wood for the stove. Upon hearing of his sister's death, Willard McCourt traveled to Denver and shared how the family had attempted to help Elizabeth on numerous occasions, but she always refused. She remained a proud woman until her death, dismissing charity; untouched clothes and food boxes were found in her cabin. Writings discovered after her passing demonstrated her stubbornness and desire to be independent.

When Elizabeth's daughter Lily was notified of her mother's death as the next of kin, Lily insisted she was the daughter of Horace's older brother, John. All relationships with the Leadville senator and widow were denied.

Several hundred local Leadville citizens came to pay their respects at Elizabeth's funeral on March 13, 1935, at the Annunciation Catholic Church. Some women reflected on her character, saying they had forgiven her past affair. Others admitted her determination to stick it out at the cabin was inspiring. The newspapers reported that she was buried in a gray casket wearing a plain brown crepe dress. New slippers were found unused in her cabin and placed daintily on her feet for her final rest. A grave was blasted out (due to the frozen soil) in the nearby St. Joseph Cemetery, but this site was not used. The once–"silver queen of Colorado" was to be buried at Mount Olivet Cemetery in Wheat Ridge, just outside Denver, outside the community that had shunned Elizabeth for the past thirty or forty years.

Top: Horace and Elizabeth "Baby Doe" Tabor's grave in the Mount Olivet Cemetery in Westminster, Colorado. *Author's collection.*

Bottom: The nickname she hated forever inscribed in stone. *Author's collection.*

With this decision, Horace's body was excavated from the abandoned Calvary Cemetery (now the location of the reportedly haunted Denver Botanical Gardens) to be moved to his new resting place next to his wife. The McCourt family paid the expenses for Elizabeth's services, but the Robert W. Speer Club funded the monument to honor the Tabors at their graves. The nickname that followed her to the grave is inscribed on her headstone: "Baby Doe."

"Her passing at Leadville has left a gap so small as scarcely to be noticed," wrote *The Rocky Mountain News* on March 11, 1935.

This was hardly the case.

Soon after, the news of Elizabeth's death spread, and despite the no-trespassing signs put up by the coroner, Elizabeth's cabin was ransacked by vandals. Anything that might have been of value was stolen. Several trunks were said to hold news clippings and photos she had kept over the years. Newspaper clippings, including ones regarding Silver Dollar's Chicago death, hint Elizabeth may have known about the tragedy to an extent. She only kept a few personal items, despite selling most of her goods to repay her debts. These items included her fur coat and silver-lined wedding dress, which thieves took. Luckily, these items were recovered. As of this writing, the coat is displayed on-site at the Matchless, while the dress is displayed in the Center for Colorado Women's History in Denver.

In the 1950s, the Leadville Assembly restored and reassembled the mine and cabin as a museum. In 1988, the Shorego Mining Company donated it to the assembly. Today, the property is maintained by the National Mining Hall of Fame and Museum. The Matchless Mine and cabin stand as a testament to mining history, along with the woman who stayed there for thirty-five years. It is too dangerous to enter the mine, but a visitor can approach the exterior entry of the shaft mine. Here, miners entered through a thin shaft, a pulley system connected to the nearby hoist house. Candlelight provided the only source of light, and the environment was hazardous due to toxic gases and the potential for injury from drilling and dynamite explosions.

When you enter the cabin, the room is set up similarly to how Elizabeth would have kept it during her time there. Some newspaper linings are still visible, while a protectant covers the walls from damage. The calendar is frozen in time, with February 21, 1935, as the last entry, never being changed since her death, which she likely prefers.

Interesting to note: she often wrote on her wall calendar, and its last inscription was one word, *spirits*, on February 21. What did this mean?

Another thing that remains the same in the cabin is the queen herself. There are stories that Elizabeth continues to keep watch at the Matchless Mine. Some staff whisper that they have odd feelings in the cabin, as if they are not alone. Shadows have been seen; lights will turn on and off. Staff have heard phantom knocks and whispers when no one else is present. There is a general warning of caution that the name "Baby Doe" should not be uttered; otherwise, there is hell to pay. Several museum guides will start their days by greeting "Mrs. Tabor" and find that they have a spectacular day without incident. It sounds as if she still demands respect, even in the afterlife.

Shane Kinney is a registrar at the National Mining Hall of Fame and Museum in Leadville. During his time with the museum, he experienced the spirit of Elizabeth. He explained:

> *I was packing up the cabin for winter storage of the artifacts. I was playing music on my phone. Whenever I tried to write the name "Baby Doe" on one of the artifact boxes, or if my coworker referred to the cabin as "Baby Doe's Cabin," the music would stop playing, and I would have to restart it. Now, this was not music running off of a data or internet connection these were songs I had downloaded on my phone. I apologized to Mrs. Tabor, knocked on her door, and asked for entry, which seemed to have calmed down the activity. I made it a habit to announce myself and knock from then on, and I have had no problems since.*

Before he started at the museum, his director had an experience. "My director told us that at a dedication ceremony for the Matchless Mine site, where there was a large sheet cake made in honor of her birthday that said, 'Happy Birthday, Baby Doe.' When the cake was revealed, a gust of wind came up and blew the cake over onto the ground; that's what I was told happened." Was Elizabeth showing her disdain by destroying the cake, or was it just a strong wind at a coincidental time?

These strange anomalies are not just experienced at the cabin. Strange oddities have occurred in the hoist house just below the cabin. Disembodied knocks and soft voices have been heard; doors have shut independently without a reasonable cause. Shane does not feel alone around the mine. "I can say it still feels busy to me like at any moment I could look around and see workers and miners, and it would all feel natural."

The legend of Baby Doe continues a century after her death, and the love/scandal story has been told through movies and two operas written

Outside the Matchless Mine, where Elizabeth Tabor lived and died alone. *Photo courtesy of Shane Kinney.*

about her life. This story has many developments and plot twists: riches-to-rags, a scandal in a booming mining town and a woman who dies destitute and alone. Many people are still horrified by the torrid affair and consequential marriage, and they feel Elizabeth found love in the wrong way. Elizabeth "Baby Doe" Tabor continues to stay on watch for her mine, which never prospered. As an ironic event, the silver cost rose a month after her death.

Some are still on the fence about their alliance with the woman who died at the mine. Did she lose her mind? Or was she a strong, independent woman who was too prideful to leave? If you decide to visit the Matchless Mine on Fryer Hill, you will want to show some respect to a woman who left a noticeable mark on history. You might not know who is listening.

4

Harrison Avenue

A Ghostly Strip

The town grew as Leadville lured miners to the area with promises of riches. Saloons, dance halls and gambling dens popped up seemingly overnight. One visitor, in 1879, remarked that it was the noisiest place during the day, but it was way worse at night. The city was bustling, crowded and dirty. East Chestnut Street was the first main road in the city before the parallel Harrison Avenue took precedence. Let us travel down the busy roads of past mining life to meet some of their forever residents.

Chestnut Street runs parallel to the rambunctious State Street, with businesses running on both the west and east sides. When the new road was named after Edwin Harrison, the premier smelter, it quickly became the main street through town. Traffic overflowed, and people slept in the streets, covered in dust and debris. Visiting Quaker lawyer George Elder wrote in 1879, "Murders occur in such a terribly reckless manner than it is uncertain who will be the next victim." Whether they died from overdose, murder, suicide or illness, there were often bodies heading to the city cemetery.

Theaters

By 1878, the city census identified 120 saloons, 19 bar halls, 35 houses of sex work (among three red-light districts) and 188 gambling halls; on the other hand, there were 4 churches, 4 banks, 31 restaurants, 10 dry goods shops and 70 law firms representing claims, according to Grim's "A Brief History of Leadville." All businesses were required to pay a licensing fee. Multiple theaters stood along the roads, welcoming audiences in for various forms of entertainment. Theaters were separated into two categories: variety and professional. The first theater was The Coliseum, which opened as a variety theater at 134 West Chestnut Street. Deaths occurred on property from illness and murder. The building was destroyed in 1881 fire, and despite multiple injuries, the only fatality was that of a pedestrian who was struck by the wagon tongue of the firetruck while it was on the way to the burning building.

Until the railroads came through town, the choice of actors was slim and limited on acting skills. For the women and children, Ben Wood and Tom Kemp opened Wood's Opera House on East Chestnut Street, where there was no alcohol and the presentation of respect for families—during the matinées anyway. Over the next few years, the opera house went through three new names before the structure was also lost in a fire. On May 19,

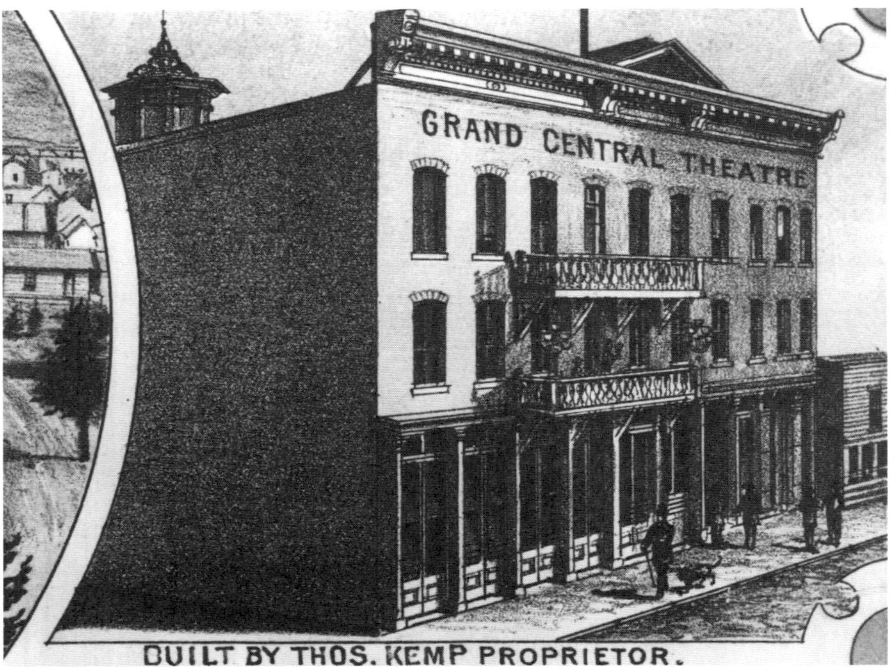

Grand Central Theatre, one of the many entertainment venues circa 1880–85. *Denver Public Library.*

The Clarendon Hotel saloon, circa 1890–95. The hotel was built in 1879 by Horace Tabor and W.H. Bush. It served as a hospital during the 1918 flu epidemic. However, love for the building fell out over the years, and it was demolished in the 1950s. Today, the lot is the location of a gas station. Perhaps past guests of the hotel linger in the lot. *Author's collection.*

1882, smoke and panic were in the air as the fire spread to the Hotel Windsor, Hotel Brunswick and the Palace of Fashion. These cases of arson led to the ultimate demise of East Chestnut Street, all left in ashes.

Theaters were abundant not only on East Chestnut Street but also on Fifth Street and Harrison Avenue. Most, if not all, were burned in fires. The last standing theater from the historic days is the three-story red brick building at 308 Harrison Avenue. The Tabor Opera House opened on Harrison Avenue in 1879, when Mr. Horace Tabor wanted the grandest theater on this side of St. Louis. The Tabor Opera House was the first building in Leadville to install gas lighting; 72 jets shone the actors' brilliance on the stage. Meanwhile, there were around 880 luxurious velvet seats for the audience and private boxes for Horace and Augusta. The stage was built with a trapdoor, rumored to be for none other than Harry Houdini, and the opera house once hosted a circus that included elephants!

The Tabor Opera House's website includes the history of its fine building. After the Silver Panic of 1893, Tabor could not pay the bank on his note, and the theater was sold to Judge A.S. Weston in 1894 for $32,000. After the judge passed away in 1897, his wife, Leticia, took over management of the Weston Opera House until she fell into foreclosure in 1899. Although the opera house had a new owner, J.W. Doyle of Cripple Creek, he allowed Mrs. Weston to carry on running its operations. Only three women in the entire country managed a theater then, and Leticia was one of them. In 1901, the local Elks Lodge purchased the building. The opera house underwent an entire remodel, with a larger stage and dressing rooms, hotel rooms, and the upper walkway from the building to the once-standing Clarendon Hotel added on. A ballroom was added to this space. Expansions were made to the auditorium. Over time, the Elks Opera House struggled through two world wars and the Great Depression. By 1955, the Elks wanted out, and a young woman named Evelyn Furman desired to save the theater from potential demolition. After convincing her mother to purchase the structure, Evelyn operated the theater for fifty-nine years. The Tabor shone once again and continues to shine, even today. As of 2016, the City of Leadville owns and operates the theater, and it offers shows and tours to anyone who would like a glimpse of the past. Visit their website for more information.

SALOONS

As mentioned previously, there were many places of entertainment in the ever-growing Leadville. Life was tough, and people wanted a place to let their hair down and relax. A few stick around, and so do their ghosts.

Driving around town now, it is hard to imagine the time of 120 bawdy saloons, dance halls and other places of fancy. As a form of entertainment, it was estimated that customers drank around 200 kegs of beer per day. At a cost of about $0.10 per drink, a bartender might make $100 per day. Women appeared in saloons as waitresses, also known as "beer juggers," earning 5 percent of every $1.

Driving north into town, a historic, original-structured saloon stands on the left side at 315 Harrison Avenue, just across from the Tabor Opera House. Built in 1883, with the name The Board of Trade, the Legendary Silver Dollar Saloon is one of the last still-standing relics of the drinking halls. The interior provides another glimpse into history, as the saloon appears much like it did 140 years ago. With original bar and tile floors, modern amenities such as televisions have been installed, of course. Here, Oscar Wilde was said to have gotten a drink or two while he was in town to perform at the opera house. Whether he drank here or at one of the other 129 saloons, he was amused to find a hanging sign: "Don't shoot the piano player, he is doing the best he can."

John "Doc" Holliday also spent time here, drinking and playing faro when he supposedly lived across the street above Hyman's saloon. Years before taking her fateful trip on the *Titanic*, Margaret Brown also spent some time within the wooden walls, her husband, J.J., at her side. At a time when social convention dictated what proper ladies said and did, a windbreak at the entrance blocked any eyes from seeing what may be occurring within the saloon walls as they passed.

The saloon apparently went through a temporary name change to the Bank Saloon; this was short-lived before it returned to the Board of Trade. By the 1930s, the name was updated to its current iteration. This beloved bar is popular and keeps customers returning, even after death. It is said that the paranormal are "alive" within the 140-year-old saloon. However, who are they? While violence and death were prevalent in the area, one known murder did occur within the Board of Trade in 1880. Richard Dillon was mortally wounded when he was shot twice during a heated card game over faro chips. Reportedly, he did not have the chance to fire the gun he was still holding when he fell, and he was carried out of the saloon to his house on

Above: Silver Dollar Saloon is home to a few spirits—and we're not talking about alcohol. *Author's collection.*

Opposite, top: A saloon with gambling machines circa 1880–1910. *Denver Public Library.*

Opposite, bottom: A saloon bar circa 1880–1910. *Denver Public Library.*

Hyman's Saloon was a popular hall circa 1882–90. *Photo by Way and Knoezer.*

West Fifth Street. Could he be one of the restless spirits hanging out and seeking justice?

According to Atlas Obscura, several unknown paranormal teams visited the saloon and declared there were at least eight spirits there. Among its relics of the past, the saloon was said to hold the noose from the last hanging in town and the shoes of a little girl who died in the old tunnels under the saloon's location. Supposedly, these deaths were related to the hauntings. Staff have experienced electrical interference and aggressive behaviors, which are said to be the behaviors of the little girl. Supposedly, staff fear entering the basement alone. This author attempted to reach the saloon for additional context but received no response.

Across the street stands the Hyman block at 314/316 Harrison Avenue. Built in 1880 next to the Tabor Opera House, the building held multiple purposes, including a cigar shop in the front, a saloon and a gambling den tucked in the back. Mannie Hyman added to the building in 1885 and completed it in 1890. The second floor had rooms for rent, and it is said that he let "Doc" Holliday stay there for free as he worked as a faro dealer at the saloon downstairs.

Former Leadville Policeman William "Bill" Allen and his buddy John Tyler reportedly had a problem with Holliday since the Tombstone days—Holliday also held a grudge. One day, Allen approached Holliday over an owed $5, which Holliday was not about to turn over. Threats ensued, including one that Holliday was about to plan his own funeral. On that eventful day in August 1884, it is said Doc had a Colt hidden in a medicine cabinet. Per city ordinance, Holliday was not allowed to have a gun on him, and he tried to obey this. On this day, Allen followed him into the saloon, and Holliday snagged the hidden weapon and took deadly aim. However, he hit Allen in the arm. Allen survived, and Holliday was charged. The owner of the Board of Trade was said to assist in his bail. Ultimately, he was acquitted of charges, except for an $8,000 fine. Holliday eventually traveled on to Glenwood Springs, where he died from tuberculosis in 1887. "This is funny," he declared, looking down at his bare feet, as he always thought he would die with his boots on.

Today, the haunted Hyman block stories are told among visitors and paranormal enthusiasts. When the Bonanza Trading Co. shop occupied the location, there was a rumor that a ghostly little boy and girl ran around the shop. The story alleges that the spirit children are related to the madam of the brothel that was said to be upstairs; however, as the space was known only as rooms for rent, it is unknown who these children may be. Perhaps they are the children of past renters or boarders. The Leadville Running Series shop stands watch today, and occupants have acknowledged hearing disembodied bumps. However, there are no reports of phantom child–like behavior. Have the children moved on to a new place to play and haunt?

HAUNTED HARRISON AVENUE

Ask people about the haunted locations in Leadville, and they will say the entire city is full of ghosts. Spirits have been experienced in not only the buildings and mines but also the streets. Of course, as you have already read, legends of the hauntings started soon after the city's development.

In 1904, on Fourth Street and Harrison Avenue, steam often rose from the mining ditches on chilly nights. One night was no exception. A mine manager was coming home from a card night at the Elks lodge. He got scared for his life, a story he would likely tell for decades. While walking, the steam was especially noticeable as he observed what looked like a large black watch hanging without support. The man watched as snow blew through the object, seemingly transparent, and as he approached it with an outstretched hand, his hand did not connect with anything solid. His

Looking north of Harrison Avenue, which is lined with telephone poles. The Tabor Opera House stands to the right, the Famous stands on the left, circa 1880–90. *Photo by William Henry Jackson.*

friend walked through the object without being aware of the anomaly. Shaking it off, the man continued along toward his home. He glanced across the street and could not believe his eyes: the jewelry store had a sizeable wooden watch outside the shop that reflected light into the steam. It was no ghost, and he was mighty relieved not to have encountered a spirit.

Not all encounters can be so easily explained.

Walking around Leadville is like traveling back in time to a colorful and rich history. Visitors can walk past Colorado's oldest Odd Fellows Hall, established in 1890. Down the block stands the Masonic lodge at 619 Harrison Avenue; the building was dedicated in 1911. The 1897 clapboard-structured Davis Drug Store operated as a drugstore and one of the many saloons in Leadville. The Stickley Insurance Building at 613 Harrison Avenue is a clapboard building with four safes from 1880 that once held precious documents. The nearby Western Hardware Store is currently an antique shop but once housed all the tools and needs for construction. Walking inside, one can see the interior structure that reflects the store's past life of a hardware business.

While walking down Harrison Avenue today, one might also pass a departed soul that the human eye cannot see. There are tales of spirits in many buildings along the avenue, not just the saloons and hotels. The Famous restaurant beside Silver Dollar has supposedly had some strange occurrences in its upstairs apartments—and not just from living tenants. The building, built in 1879 or 1880, housed many businesses, such as a drugstore, a china shop and a bank.

During the Upper Chestnut days in 1880, a couple of miners were heading home to their cabin on Carbonite Hill. It was a chilly October night, so it was odd when they saw a man without a hat or coat. When the moonlight struck the man's face, the miners were chilled to the bone to see a "pale and bloody face, with a hole where one eye should have been," according to author Roger Pretti. These witnesses were not the only ones who saw the spirit of Richard Stephenson, who had been killed at the Miner's Arms Saloon the previous month. Stephenson came to Leadville after his new wife, Hattie McGran (or McGrann), fled to her mother's home due to his relationship with alcohol and his failure to provide for the home. When Richard arrived at Hattie's mother's boardinghouse in Cloud City, Hattie refused his advances. Instead of leaving town, he found work at one of the local hotels. Here, he learned of his wife's rendezvous with other men around town, including the dashing Thomas Morgan. Fueled by anger, on

September 9, 1880, Stephenson loaded up on booze at the saloon while waiting for the man who'd caught Hattie's eye.

Morgan was in and out of the saloon, buying rounds for others. After he left again, Stephenson asked the bartender, "Lend me a gun, will you?" But he was denied. Morgan came back into the bar, declaring, "Damn you, you [expletive]—I've got you now!" Morgan pointed a pistol at the drunk husband's face, and he was not fast enough to move from danger. Stephenson fell as Morgan fired the fatal bullet. A reporter from the *Carbonate Chronicle* was allowed access to the mortuary to see the body of the deceased; there was a hole where an eye should have been. The body was buried in the Evergreen Cemetery two days later. Like Upper Chestnut Street, the Miner's Arms Saloon is long gone. Roger Pretti stated that on October nights, the spirit continues walking in the vacant field where the busy road once flourished, "caught somewhere between Leadville and the next world." The forlorn spirit still eternally pursues the wife who is forever gone to him.

The Tabor House Museum is a step off Harrison Avenue on Fifth Street. When Horace and Augusta moved to Leadville, they lived on a plot of land near 308 Harrison Avenue. When the idea of an opera house popped into his mind, Horace decided that the perfect spot was precisely where his current home was. So, he moved his house to the offshoot of Fifth Avenue. Horace and Augusta lived here until 1881, when he moved his mistress into the Clarendon Hotel. Today, the house stands as a museum. Some whisperings say spiritual remnants of the Tabors (excluding Elizabeth "Baby Doe") have stayed in the old home in some form. Are these rumors or memories like a recorded videotape replaying over time?

The Tabor House Museum is where Horace and Augusta once lived. *Author's collection.*

A sketch depiction of the theater, circa 1881. *Denver Public Library.*

Now we'll move over the following block to the house at 114 West Sixth Street, where a spirit appeared to a couple at the back of their apartment one evening in March 1880. According to Roger Pretti, an apparition of "a man in a long, black coat and a hat, standing by the stove" disappeared after the couple demanded to know who he was and why he was in their home. The spirit reappeared shortly after a series of questionable gunshots and screams infiltrated the air outside the home. The spirit asked the couple, "What's the matter?" And then he stepped out onto the street and vanished again.

It seems like there is something spooky on every block.

Cookies with an Altitude, located at 717 Harrison Avenue, had a ghostly woman in its kitchen. According to owner Sherry Randall, "It felt like definitely a presence trying to communicate." Hanging beads in a doorway had been seen swaying as if touched by an invisible hand, and Sherry's baking spoons rocked on their racks without a reasonable draft causing them to do so.

Sherry gathered a small group of participants to hold a ghost hunt at the building. Using a communication device, the group was surprised to learn that the female spirit had once worked in the building. The word *bodies* was spit from the communication device. The building for *The Herald Democrat* was and still is located in the same structure and once briefly housed an undertaker's business. M.A. Buxton was the successor for the town's oldest mortuary establishment, James Nelson's Undertakers, when he moved the business to this location from 607 Harrison Avenue. So, it might make sense for the past mortuary to have strange anomalies.

According to a 2017 article in *The Herald Democrat*, a previous newspaper editor reportedly heard loud noises coming from the basement and lights turning on without a physical touch. At the time, no one was present besides the editor. It was speculated that one of the building's ghosts may have been a former newspaper editor, and this was later confirmed by the ghost hunter's communication devices.

The name came out of nowhere. A friendly stray cat taught Sherry that the female spirit was named Mollie (or Molly, as the spelling is unknown). Over time, the living and dead became kindred spirits.

In 2019, Cookies with an Altitude evolved into the Silver Llama Market and Eatery when it moved locations to 615 Harrison Avenue. Strangely enough, the Leadville Occult Society held a parlor and lecture meeting at this address when the structure served as a hall for the Patriotic Order Sons of America (POS of A). This fraternal group was for young men aged sixteen to twenty-one, devised from the Masonic Order. The location previously served as a drugstore before it became the development that stands today. The building was renovated in the last decade after the roof collapsed from the elements, but could old energy still be sticking around? The answer is yes. Mollie and her friends continued visiting Sherry in her new location.

"She comes to visit my shop," Sherry explained, saying that she saw unexplainable things occurring via her security camera. When no one was present, objects fell off the counters without reason. One day, one of the cooks nervously approached and encouraged Sherry to look at the cameras. "Something fell off the counter...like somebody walked through the kitchen behind him and started knocking things off." The staff member noted the time and calmly left the kitchen to alert his employer.

The spirits appear to be friendly. Sherry says there are plenty at both locations.

While he was still relatively wealthy, Horace Tabor was busy investing in the city's glamour. He hired George E. King to design a grand hotel, the aptly named Tabor Grand Hotel, at the corner of Seventh Street and Harrison Avenue. Built in 1885, this fine hotel had the only hydraulic elevator in town. Here, Elizabeth Tabor sat in an eccentric offset perch in the building; she was thought to be counting the ore cars that came down Seventh Avenue from the Matchless. Each mine cart needed to be accounted for as it traveled down to the assayer and smelter. That was money, after all. After the Panic of 1893 occurred, the four-story building was sold and renovated into the Maxwell, then the Kitchen Brothers, followed by the Vendome Hotel. Constructed in the Victorian style, the building is adorned with a central tower, roof cresting and dormer windows. According to Leadville by Lamplight tour guide Rhone Pretti, there has been a sighting of a woman in black here. Could she be related to the female spirit in black that is rumored to haunt the mining district? Rhone believes this may be Elizabeth, possibly "mourning her lavish life or her husband who died." Perhaps she waits for the ore cars to come down the hill again. As it was traditional for Victorians to don black clothing while in mourning, this woman does appear to be grieving—who or what she might be grieving, we do not know for sure. Besides the woman in black, there have also been reports of spirit children playing with toys in the halls of the once-monumental hotel. This historic haunted building holds thirty-seven affordable apartments, shops and offices today.

Author's note: Up Seventh Street, at 609 Poplar Street, stands the 1880 Annunciation Catholic Church. This was the location of J.J. and Margaret Brown's wedding in 1886… and Elizabeth Tabor's funeral in 1935.

Passing the Tabor Grand, let us head up to Capitol Hill; the name stuck when Leadville was vying to become the location of the state capitol. Instead of erecting a government building here, the Leadville High School was constructed in 1900. Today, the building is the National Mining Hall of Fame and Museum. The expansive brick building still houses the school's old classrooms, appearing as they once did; pale green paint adorns the walls, chalk scribblings lace the boards and desks still wait for long-since-gone pupils to learn new topics. Shane Kinney works at the museum and explained, "I've personally seen moving shadows throughout the building, which a few of the other staff members have seen." He has been curious about who has been creeping around. Is school still in session? Are the shadows the spirits of students or teachers? It remains a mystery.

Perhaps the spirits are visitors from an otherworldly Leadville. One night, in the distant past, the museum was hosting an event at the Matchless Mine. The event, Spirits at the Shaft, was a success, guided by a medium named Sarah. After the event's conclusion, the staff retreated to the mining museum to unwind and discuss the night's activities. A staff member had dressed up as Elizabeth "Baby Doe" Tabor and returned to the museum while still in costume. Sarah shifted her attention to the woman, stating that a male spirit had come through. Local Sherry Randolph recalled that the medium told

A classroom looks like it's still ready for students. Leadville High School is now the National Mining Hall of Fame. *Photo courtesy of Shane Kinney.*

the Baby Doe doppelgänger, "There is a man here who says you look just as beautiful as the day you met." Within moments, the male caller was said to be none other than Horace Tabor. The man and legend had made his way to the old school, seeking the energy of the woman he loved until his death. Perhaps some Cloud City spirits travel around the town that was and is still home, much like they did in life.

These are only a few ghost stories from this historic stretch of Leadville. There are other tracings of hauntings within residences and museums, which may include a shadow here and there or a disembodied sound that is never to be repeated. So much life was lived along this avenue; you can feel the energy in the air. Some of that energy may be attached to the building, physical items or people. Just walk along the sidewalks and tune out the noise of today; walk in the footsteps of those before us. Perhaps one will tell you of their story.

5

DELAWARE HOTEL

SOME NEVER CHECK OUT

After the Windsor and Clarendon Hotels were established and became busy with clientele, the Delaware Hotel was built on Harrison Avenue in 1883 to attract affluent guests and cater to all their needs. The hotel is one of the few historic buildings you can visit and sleep at in Leadville, and it's brimming with history…and spirits.

In 1880, the Leadville's population swelled to thirty thousand. The main street was full of hotels, boardinghouses and gambling halls. The working men lived and worked in the mines and played harder along Harrison Avenue and State Street. The streets were getting rowdy, and those higher up the social ladder peered down their noses at the revelers. People like Horace Tabor wanted Leadville to be known as a civilized town.

In 1883, three brothers from Delaware funded a brand-new hotel with $80,000. Making their money from Denver shops, William, George and John Callaway named the hotel as a tribute to their home state. George King designed the building. The elite hotel was built to beckon wealthy visitors to stay in town.

One marketing tactic was to boast the washrooms on each floor, shared among fifty guest rooms. Guests would not be in the dark either; gas-illuminated light fixtures were a new novelty. Those who spent more had rooms with a private toilet, not to be shared with strangers. Hot and cold water flowed through the taps. Guests were to be well pampered at the Delaware. (The basement still has the well that was used to pump water into the hotel.)

The Delaware Hotel in its historical glory, circa 1900–10. *Denver Public Library.*

One famous guest who was rumored to have stayed at the Delaware Hotel was O.K. Corral gunslinger John "Doc" Holliday. Holliday spent some time in the Cloud City and was rumored to have stayed on the hotel's third floor. He was often in trouble and kept a room on the third floor that overlooked Harrison Avenue. This way, if the lawmen were coming toward the hotel, he could make a break for it by jumping out the window and into the next-door firehouse. Doc may have stayed hidden in this room after his death. After making jokes at the spirits' expense, a guest later claimed they met Doc's spirit in the room. They were a believer after that encounter!

By 1887, more men were becoming overnight millionaires from silver production. The town's population continued to grow, with more people wanting to get their hands on the precious metal. The Callaway brothers decided to close their ground-floor shop at the hotel and leased it as a dry supply store. Over the next decade, the railroads transported millions of pieces of silver ore to Denver. Then the money train stopped when silver lost its value; this marked the beginning of the Silver Panic of 1893, a period that would test the resilience of the Delaware Hotel.

During the crash, many businesses went bankrupt or closed altogether. The Callaways were savvy during this time, reducing the cost of rent in the building for shops and rooms, and this kept the Delaware from closing. The Callaways retired from managing the block in 1940 (or 1946, depending on the source) by selling it for $40,000. Over the next few decades, the building went through a few owners. By 1986, the building had been reopened as a hotel and boardinghouse for extended stays. Gone were the days of shops located on the ground floor, as the first floor was renovated in 1992 to hold a spacious lobby. When the Williamses purchased the building in 2000, the married couple brought the Victorian past back to life with a fresh remodel.

Today, the hotel is under new management. The new owners continue to renovate and restore the historic building, with a new bar, restaurant and ice cream shop currently in the works. The forty hotel rooms are refurbished with modern amenities, and guests are no longer expected to share washrooms. Upon checking in, guests venture up a staircase to reach the second floor. There is no current elevator, so if a guest has a third-floor room, there is another grand stairwell. Pack lightly.

Now, guests may have private rooms, but they may not be alone. The Delaware is said to be home to several spirits. The most popular spirit in the hotel is that of Mary Gallagher Coffey. Mary and her husband, Jerry, traveled to Leadville with their children (out of six children, only two survived). Jerry was always jealous and abusive to his wife from early on in the relationship. One day, she was beaten with a candlestick. Jerry was arrested but did not stay locked up for long. In a cycle of what seemed to be abuse, Jerry behaved for a while before he struck again. In April 1889, Jerry accused Mary of infidelity and had her arrested for adultery. He later withdrew his conviction.

Above: The hotel lobby of the Delaware Hotel. *Author's collection.*

Opposite: Mary Coffey's room, where she was staying when she was shot by her husband. *Author's collection.*

By July, Jerry had acted out again. Police were called for the assault, and he shot twice at Officer John Morgan with the same gun he later used in Mary's murder. Consequently, he was arrested, but he was released after a few weeks. Mary took cover with their children at the Delaware Hotel in October 1889. Again, she let Jerry back into their lives. Around midnight on November 3, 1889, she returned to room 5 after helping a sick friend in another room. Fueled by anger, Jerry accused Mary of being unfaithful and cried out, "I'll fix you now!" Mary started to walk away, but Jerry shot her in the back—and then shot her again after she fell. Mary was paralyzed from the waist down, and despite what could only be unimaginable pain, she was able to tell the officers what happened. Jerry was found outside after he hid the pistol in the washroom. He told the sheriff one of these two phrases (as reported in the local newspapers): "She harassed the life out of me!" or "She harassed me to death!"

Over the next two days, the children watched their mother die. Mary died on November 6, 1889, and was interred at the City Cemetery using funds

donated by some of the local women of Leadville. Jerry was charged and served a life sentence at Colorado Territorial Prison. However, Mary continues to grace the hotel where she lived her final moments. She is seen as a woman in a blue dress or a wispy woman in white and seems to take care of the hotel's guests. What is more, she is seen only from the waist up. Sometimes, guests staying in room 203 have claimed Mary visits them; others have seen Mary standing in the window.

Roger Pretti has written about other spirits that play around the hotel, such as Billy, a child-like ghost. Per legend, he was an orphan who liked to spend his time messing with guests. On one occasion, two hotel staff members were idly telling ghost stories when Billy was mentioned as a mischievous spirit. To make a believer in his friend, the man asked the child spirit to turn off the lights of a nearby chandelier. Almost immediately, the light fixture went dark. There was no indirect way to turn off the lights. While Billy is said to play throughout the hotel, he is attached to room 329. If you bring him toys like marbles, he might play with you.

As they do at many other hotels, some people check in, never to walk out alive. Other deaths were rumored to have occurred in the hotel, although these are challenging to confirm. Still, ghost stories remained, such as that of Cornelia; the nine-year-old's life was cut short by sudden pneumonia. Her spirit is said to be in room 202 and will close doors on unsuspecting guests.

Miner William Ellison died from a hemorrhage in room 320, and his spirit will allegedly steal guests' things. In room 318, Hattie Oglethorpe died by suicide in 1888; it is said that she was waiting forever for her love to return from the mines. The downstairs area, near the newer restaurant in the building, is haunted by an old pioneer named Kenai Davis, who passed away in his hotel room from an extended illness.

The hotel embraces its ghostly residents and will share experiences that have been had there. The current manager, Yasmine, expressed that the new

The second floor of the Delaware Hotel. *Author's collection.*

restaurant has given her odd feelings, especially later at night. Perhaps she has been experiencing the spirit of the old pioneer?

Yasmine suspects one of the Callaway brothers is still watching over the business. His office was located downstairs, and occasionally, visitors still catch the smell of cigar smoke. Now, smoking is not allowed in any Colorado business, so is it possible that a spirit could still be lighting one up? This could also be a residual haunting, an etching of the past disguised as an olfactory sensation.

Many who renovate old buildings often experience an uproar from ghosts not impressed with their changes. This is true for the Delaware, which has undergone recent renovations. Workers who stayed on site to assist with getting the job completed complained of their sleep being disturbed. One of the painters felt a burst of cold air rush by him. Terrified, he packed up his equipment and fled the building. Another time, there was a splashing event downstairs that the workers witnessed together. They were met with a flooded floor. There was no specific reason for the water spill.

After the renovations were complete, one guest had quite a problem in her bathroom. She came downstairs to complain. The water in the toilet bowl was *hot and steaming*. A plumber looked it over and could not explain the cooked water. Having enough of the spirits' outbursts, the hotel owner spoke to the open air for anyone to listen. He explained that he just wanted the hotel to be impressive and beautiful. This seemed to do the trick, as the activity stopped.

Some guests may still awaken to odd noises and creaks in the early morning, especially on the top floor. Here, a tragic scene occurred almost seventy-five years prior. In the early morning of April 8, 1949, Officer William Mindenhall witnessed a man trying to break into a car. The suspect brandished a gun, which led the officer to call his night captain. Officer Alvin Nelson met with Officer Mindenhall around 3:30 a.m. and found the car thief packing bags in his third-floor room at the Delaware. It should be noted that other reports indicated the suspect was attempting to only flee officers when they encountered him on the top floor.

As they tried to arrest him, the suspect, Arvin Wurts, shot twice at Officer Nelson and killed him. Officer Mindenhall returned fire and killed the suspect; this was later determined to have been done in self-defense. The kicker was that Officer Nelson had only been filling in for the night. He had recently retired as night police chief to return to patrol work. Could the trauma from the event be the cause of some of the activity? It is hard to tell in a hotel that saw so much life and death.

Exterior painting on the Delaware Hotel. *Author's collection.*

Over the years, the spirits of the Delaware have engaged in other ways, such as creating knocks, creaks or disembodied voices that float from empty rooms. An overnight desk clerk received a wake-up call, which was not unusual. What was unusual was that the caller said she was Mary Coffey and that she needed to be woken to check out at 7:00 a.m. The call came from room 2, which was not booked for that night. In 2024, a skeptical guest was made a believer after they claimed a blueish orb floated across their room in the early morning hours. Another person reported hearing a noise, as if an unseen entity was walking through their room. Paranormal enthusiasts will stay up all night to witness any activity. There is no significant pattern; it appears that the spirits engage on their own ghostly schedule.

Visit the Delaware Hotel at 700 Harrison Avenue, stay the night and keep an eye (and ear) open. The hotel boasts Victorian charm with updated washrooms in each room. While the staff embraces the spirits, the spirits play host to the living guests. If you are lucky, you may see an apparition of one of the phantom guests. They are not malicious; they want to be seen and heard. Stay the night—they stay forever.

6

Spirits of the Red-Light District

Returning to the discovery of silver in 1877, the not-yet-named city, or "Slabtown," as Horace Tabor referred to the area, started filling with people from all over, those who wanted to try their hands at making it rich in the mines and those who were more than happy to take the money out of others' hands. Along the town's busy main streets, many businesses, such as saloons, eateries and boardinghouses, popped up to cater to the people. Then there were the ladies who catered to men, divided by areas of town. Often, love and lust were confused, especially when alcohol was added to the mix. Many brothels in the district no longer stand, but the spirits of ladies from the past may still have the red light on.

During the town's boom days, Leadville was male-oriented, and few respected women lived in the community. Finding jobs outside of laundry and boardinghouses was tough; some women went to the bawdier side of town. In 1879, Leadville was full of brothels with women who were more than happy to be paid to take on the role of companion, especially when the men spent their time at one of the town's more than one hundred saloons or gambling halls. The cribs were located on State Street (now Second Street), while the higher-paid "soiled doves" were found a short walk away on Fifth Street.

STATE STREET

The Pioneer Club was opened in 1878 on Chestnut Street as a gaming saloon before it was relocated to 118 State Street a year later. Men who visited the establishment could play anything from card games to billiards or "ten pins," which we know as bowling. Upstairs, rooms were available for newcomers who needed a place to sleep or a room for other business. A fire ripped through the building one spring night in 1892, with the upstairs residents of the so-called lodging having to flee for their lives, some in only their skivvies. The saloon and dance hall were destroyed, along with five other buildings in the vicinity. The Pioneer did not take long to rise from the ashes and rebuild at nearly the exact same location.

According to author Roger Pretti, the gas-lit streetlights were said to have "led the curious and crafty into an underworld that rivaled New York and Paris." While State Street and the Pioneer were often stages for violence, the Pioneer was also the scene of an incident in which business and love went wrong in 1889. A soiled dove named Frankie Dodge was upset that Henry Williams was leaving her. She brandished a gun and shot at him several times until one bullet connected. He died of his injury three days later. She said Williams had promised her the world, and yet he spent all his money on gambling and other ladies. She wanted to end the relationship, but he always wooed her back. A jury of sympathetic men saw this as a killing done in self-defense, as she said she shot him because the deceitful man had waived his razor toward her. Moreover, Frankie was acquitted of her charge. The judgment also might have been swayed by her beauty.

The Pioneer was the last active brothel in Leadville, closing in 1970. The last madam was Hazel "Ma" Brown. Wearing cat-eye glasses, she watched over her girls while raising her grandson. Described as a "stickler," Ma tended to the bar while her girls tended to business upstairs. She required all of the women to have regular, routine medical appointments. Despite this, Ma was charitable, giving toys to the local fire department for their toy drives, donating funds for animal welfare and hosting big holiday meals. Ma was said to not care for local law enforcement, paying them off to turn their heads away from the Pioneer. After Ma's death, the two-story brick building has since been renovated to house condos. The bricks still have the name "Pioneer" etched in them, along with the date of 1892. While there are no published accounts of spirits, it could be suggested that someone is/was still attached.

State Street, circa 1880–85. *Photo by George Wakely.*

The Pioneer as it appears today. *Author's collection.*

The Pastime Bar and Pioneer are only a couple of the buildings on State Street that still stand today. *Author's collection.*

Next door to the Pioneer stands the Pastime Bar at 120 West Second Street. Built in 1879, it is one of the last standing bars from the State Street heydays. The structure held various businesses. At one time or another, it served as a brothel and theater and once held wrestling events. Law enforcement looked the other way during Prohibition, as liquor continued to flow out of the establishment. It was easy to buy your way past the law.

Most of the State Street area was dirty and known to be dangerous. Supposedly, at one time, there were about two hundred sex workers on State Street working in the brothels, not including the street girls or those up in the nicer houses. There was variety in the lower red-light district.

Along State Street was a section for white sex workers and French workers, French Row; while Black workers could be found on what was named Coon Row (a reference to a racial pejorative). The French workers had a bit of a different work ethic. The ladies were said to be clean and kept. While they did not speak much English, they were offended by vulgar language and preferred male callers to not be under the influence of alcohol. According to author Jan MacKell Collins, they "were also disgusted with American prostitutes whom they regarded as drunken, disrespectful slobs."

Stillborn Alley was located near the State Street cribs, between Harrison Avenue and Pine Street, a throughway from State to Chestnut Streets. The alley gained its name from the many infants who were found abandoned and deceased along it, although other lifeless adults and children were also often found in the alleyways. The causes of these deaths were unknown, but some citizens were concerned about infanticide. Women might not have wanted nor been able to care for a baby. Children were abundant, and only one-third of the city's children were enrolled in school. Many others worked in the mines or learned how to survive on the streets.

Behind the Pioneer Club was a twenty-foot stretch of Tiger Alley. It was likely named after the gambling halls, as gambling was known as "bucking the tiger." This was the bad news alley, and locals knew to walk on the other side of the street at night if they had to be out at all. Most carried a personal weapon. It was as easy to be murdered as it was to be robbed. While deviants were rampant in the town, footpads liked to hold up victims in the dark alleys. There, they waited to threaten someone with their pistol and before they ran back into the night.

Tiger Alley as it appears today. *Author's collection.*

Sometimes, a man could be robbed merely because he drank too much and fell back into an alley to sleep the spirits away. Newcomers to Leadville were obliviously unfamiliar with the area's notoriety. Here, padfoots were said to sneak in and rob the man as quickly as they came in. The newspaper often compared these thieves to creatures of the night as these men swooped in over State Street. An 1897 article in the *Leadville Daily/Evening Chronicle* on "positive facts" clearly stated, "The State Street vampire is invincible." Often, the very much alive thief was not caught. These thieves lurked only at night and preyed on unsuspecting or unconscious victims. The violated men were left for dead, but it was not uncommon to find a man dead from the drink or frozen to death.

In 1901, a State Street tamale salesman named Oscar Bogel was murdered in Tiger Alley in what was said to be a robbery gone wrong. The attack was said to be a bloody assault, and Oscar's body had to be identified by others who knew the man from his food cart. Some started to speculate that the murdered man had been misidentified; there was an Oscar Bogel in Mexico. Two men were charged and convicted of the crime.

Deaths by suicide were frequent occurrences in the State Street alleys. Morphine, or laudanum, was a popular drug, especially among the ladies of ill repute. Sometimes, a death occurred as a result of overdose. "A Dance of Death," ran the headline of the *Carbonate Chronicle* on November 23, 1889, after a woman from the red-light district died. Possibly sick with pneumonia, she said she would rather die. Her friends said she was a good girl and had made suicidal comments recently, but they thought she was joking. Frankie's death was listed as a result of suicide.

One unknown onlooker reflected that it did not matter how many of these women died; there was always "a perfect scramble to fill their places" in a customer's bed.

In November 1914, a fire broke out, destroying Leadville's red-light district. Twenty-two buildings on State Street were lost or damaged from the Pioneer Club down the block. The brick of the Pioneer's façade helped save the legendary brothel. The loss was estimated to be about $20,000, which is approximately $613,000 today. It was not easy to rebuild, and within a year, the district attorney Barney Whatley ordered the closure of State Street. His concern included a lack of convictions, like when a murderer was acquitted by reason of self-defense. By October 9, 1915, all residents of the "toughest little section of all of America" had vacated Leadville—all those except for the Pioneer Club women, who left the red light on.

FIFTH STREET HIGH-LIFE

The ladies of the higher class were located three blocks up from the rough and tough State Street. Initially, the neighborhood comprised the 100 block of West Park Street, later renamed Fifth Street, as the parallel streets were numbered (and State Street became Second Street). These filles de joie were considered worth the extra pay. Despite their reputation, there was drama among the ladies.

Several mansions were known to be the highbrow versions of the town's ill-reputed brothels, and many were quick to look away from the depravity. Since sex work was not legal—and therefore could not be taxed—there was a verbal agreement that the police would not raid these mansions as long as they made monthly payments to the police. Rates were fifteen dollars for the madams and five dollars for boarders. This income provided a salary for the city police, and when the payments were delayed, there was forced action.

In 1880, police raided four houses of ill repute in the upper red-light district at midnight. The residents of Frankie Paige, Sally Purple, Mollie May and Carrie Linnell were caught by surprise that night, as they were told to get dressed before they were escorted to jail. Gentlemen callers were also brought in but assumed aliases. The raid was done to make an example of the brothels, as the police were tired of the girls postponing their payments that were due on the twentieth day of every month, which affected their pay.

The white women here had more social value than those on State Street, as it was noted in 1881 that if the grand jury indicted the women on Coon Row, they would have to do the same for the women in the higher-class brothels. Laws were looser on the higher-numbered streets—except when fines were collected and domestic disturbances were intercepted.

Mollie May and Sally Purple lived next to each other on West Fifth Street, at 129 and 131, respectively, and both were madams in the trade. Winnie Purdy's "ladies' boardinghouse" was listed at 118 West Fifth Street, across from Mollie's and Sally's bordellos. The structure is long gone, now the location of a court parking lot.

Not much is known about Sally, but one thing that came up was her attitude. In 1881, she had choice words with a young man and then chased him into a store with a horsewhip. The man was struck twice in the face before the business owner intervened.

Mollie (previously known as Jennie Mickie or Mollie Mickie) was a formidable woman in her own right. She was born in 1850 or 1851 in Virginia and followed a man to Cheyenne, Wyoming, where he promptly abandoned her. This is where she met theater owner Jim McDaniels and started working as a traveling sex worker. Soon, the pair moved up to Deadwood when Jim moved his show, and Mollie followed without other plans. What a life she had survived in the badlands. She first survived a bullet hitting her corset after brothers Jim and Boone May fought for her attention. After the fight, neither man wanted anything to do with her, but Mollie adopted their last name for herself. A barfight with another sex worker, Fannie Garretson, over banjo player and Fannie's husband, Dick Brown, left Mollie's ear partially chewed off. This was too much for Mollie to take, and she left for Colorado. First, she stayed in Silver Cliffe and Bonanza before she found her way to Cloud City. When she was thirty years old, in 1878, she moved to Leadville, where she started her first bordello. An 1880 census recorded ten residents and two male employees there. She sold the house to city hall in 1881 and moved her girls to Fifth Street; it was said she had the only telephone in the city.

Mollie was often involved in altercations and especially despised her neighbor Sally Purple. Both were known for not being afraid to fight or pull a gun. Reportedly, there was one occasion in which an argument over the more remarkable birthplace escalated from spitting words to firing lead. Bullets were sprayed for two hours, but neither was hit. Reports across sources on Mollie's life said that the two women needed to rest their arms before they tried again later.

Police were often called due to domestic arguments, fights and other loudness from Mollie, her girls, her customers and even passersby. In 1880, James Burns was shot by James Langan; Burns was heading to Mollie's as he crossed Langan's property. He was taken inside the bordello, where a doctor was called, but it was too late. He died in the house.

Tensions soared when Annie Layton was accused of stealing a dress. The case was taken to a judge, and Annie thought this was a good time to interject Mollie's profession as a madame. Mollie retorted by claiming that Annie was one of her girls. The charges were dismissed.

Mollie was no stranger to the police. Once, after getting wickedly intoxicated in 1883, she claimed she was above the law, and this was followed by a punch at an officer. It took five strong officers to bring her down, and she spent the night in jail. Her girls often got into fights with other sex workers, such as when Mollie's girl Lou Ward, who was chased into the house by Kittie Sheedy. According to author Jan MacKell Collins, Lou was "slashed several times before Mollie was able to break the girls up." Mollie also had other occasions of being involved in physical altercations, robbed or assaulted. Life was rough for the Fifth Street madame.

However, she also had a softer side. By 1882, it was rumored that she had "purchased" a three-year-old daughter named Ella Moore from Utah; the adoption led the city's religious rumor mill to run amok with wagging tongues. Sick of the gossip, Mollie went to the newspaper to give an exclusive. She claimed that the child's mother was poverty-stricken and unable to care for her appropriately. Mollie quieted the running mouths by reminding locals that she often contributed to local charities. As Ella Moore was old enough for school, she was sent out east for an education.

Rumored to have a special spot for children, Mollie later came home from Utah with another three-year-old child. The mother was on the train en route to take her daughter to a poor house. The mother could not care for the child, as she had left her husband when he came home with a new wife. The child was initially to be adopted, but the adoption fell through. Mollie found the child pretty and offered to take her to Leadville. The child went through several caregivers before a local couple officially adopted her. "Children, it seemed, could always find shelter with the kindhearted Mollie May," wrote MacKell Collins.

Mollie died on April 11, 1887, from neuralgia of the heart. Her daughter was still out east and was too young to handle the funeral and estate as Mollie's next of kin. The death shook the community, as Mollie was remembered for her contributions around town. Citizens came together to throw a grand funeral. On April 13, 1887, Mollie's body was moved from her house at 129 West Fifth Street to Evergreen Cemetery in a hearse that was said to have cost $3,000 as one of the finest vehicles in town. The long procession of mourners also included two new carriages at an estimated $1,300 each. The grief-stricken friends donated flowers, and the display covered the coffin that cost "several hundreds of dollars." The *Leadville Daily/Evening Chronicle* described the special event in detail: "The notable landlady sleeps beneath the mound." The red-light district dimmed a little after her passing.

As for little Ella Moore, the newspapers indicated that she was being cared for by a foster mother who absolutely adored the little girl. It was hoped that Ella would receive the money from the estate sales. Fourteen years later, in 1901, a woman by the name Lillian Moore, said to be the daughter of Mollie, returned to Leadville, where she attempted to end her

The tree that stands over the grave of Mollie May. *Author's collection.*

own life by overdosing on cocaine. She was unsuccessful, as the newspapers reported that after she received medical treatment, the woman packed up and headed to Denver. Just like a ghost, she was never heard from again.

After Mollie's death, her spirit started appearing in her old house over the months and years. She was seen in the mirror, looking over the girls while they slept. Some suggested that Mollie was upset because her grave was not maintained with fresh flowers; others speculated that someone had taken her priceless jewelry, which was claimed to be missing from the house. Belle Jewel had taken over as house proprietor upon Mollie's passing. The newspaper reported on one occasion, Belle heard a knock at the bedroom door, only to find no one. Feeling a cold draft enter her room, she nervously knew that a spirit was looking for something in the room, which must have been Mollie. "Still on the search for her sparklers," said tour guide Rhone Pretti. The house is long gone, but is Mollie?

Today, her grave is unmarked by a tombstone or monument. However, if you know where to look, you will find her grave directly underneath a large evergreen tree in the Protestant section of the Evergreen Cemetery. The tree was her wish. The Friends of the Evergreen Cemetery tends to the entire cemetery, leaving us to wonder if Mollie is pleased with how her grave appears today.

State Street and West Fifth Street kept the red light illuminated after Mollie's death. The famed Salida sex worker Laura Evens (also documented as "Evans") started her work in Leadville in 1895, learning the job on State Street. Aware the girls up on Fifth Street made more money, she worked her way into the higher-class bordellos. Author Jan MacKell Collins wrote about an occasion when Laura caught the eye of Cripple Creek millionaire Winfield Scott Stratton, who mistook her for a societal girl when he decided to buy her a dress. While she tried on the dress, the worker informed the businessman of her status. Stratton did not mind, as he employed her time for a reputed fifty dollars.

During the miners' strike in 1896, Laura was hired to conceal the payroll to the Maid of Erin Mine, where Union strikers were blocking access. The strikers allowed Laura to pass, not suspecting the big payout that was hidden in her bustle, "'a heavy corduroy riding skirt, you know a double skirt, a voluminous thing," as Laura was quoted as saying. As the labor strikes ended, so did Laura's time in Leadville.

A Mysterious Haunting

Two houses on Front Street, located about two blocks from our red-light district, stood on an interesting side of the neighborhood. The first appearance of an apparition occurred at 604 Front Street, where a "real live ghost" terrified a woman, her adult daughter and several children. The first sighting was of a man gliding toward two children playing in the yard. The daughter, Mrs. Gleason (unknown first name, as written in the newspaper), was in terrible health, which some attributed to the ghostly occurrences. An apparition of a man appeared to her at least twice, and footsteps occurred almost nightly. On one evening, Mrs. Gleason retired to bed when the spirit entered her room and glided toward her. She tried what she could to avoid the confrontation. According to an 1883 article in *The Carbonate Chronicle*, the spirit "seized her roughly…picked her up and threw her across the room near the floor." Mrs. Gleason survived and was encouraged by a priest to vacate the house. While she was thought to have been mentally ill, others in the house validated Mrs. Gleason's experiences by agreeing that nightly footsteps from an unknown entity plagued them. What happened after the family moved out is also mysterious; there have not been any additional reports of a haunting at this location.

In 1907, another ghost tormented renters in a house at 123 Front Street. The landlord told the newspaper that two men had initially paid their lodgings in full but fled the house before their three-week time was up, blaming strange occurrences. John Wagner, who lived on Third Street, reflected on the men who were terrified of a haunting. Four nights after the men moved in, a headless man joined them for dinner. "He took a seat at the table and partook of their meal, the food he ate disappearing as he raised it to the position where his mouth would be were he to possess a head," reported *The Herald Democrat* newspaper. When the frightened men approached the entity, the headless specter vanished as suddenly as it appeared. Three days later, the headless man appeared in their bed. The scared men fled from the house to stay with a neighbor before they moved out the next day.

Wagner told *The Herald Democrat* that there was a rumor of a man who had hanged himself with his suspenders in the house "some years ago." The rumors of the haunted house spread when, a few days later, on April 11, 1907, self-proclaimed "fortune teller, spiritualistic medium and professional ghost tamer" "Prof." Herman DeMongue entered the local real estate office, tasked with finding new residents for the house on Front Street. He claimed the spirits were dissatisfied and offered to cleanse the house for $2.50 an hour. The agent Walter Stickley offered to rent it to DeMongue for $1.50 a month and said he could work to "practice on the spirit until his heart's content." DeMongue refused, and Stickley declined to pay for the so-called medium to "satisfy" the spirits.

A week later, a neighborhood teenage boy who was walking by the house, trying to impress his date, was terrified to see a flash of light coming from the house. The light was bright at first; then it dimmed, and a "man shot out…[carrying] a huge burning object in his hand, which gave worth an offensive smell." The man ran past the frightened young man across the street before dropping the ball and disappearing. The burning ball vanished as well. The boy was unsure if the man had a head, as he claimed he did not think to look in all the hubbub.

What is interesting is that this is the last of the reported hauntings. In 2020, Katie Rudolph, on behalf of the Denver Public Library, noted that the newspaper seemed to lose interest in the hauntings at 123 Front Street. There is no indication of a death by suicide occurring there, nor is there any indication of the house existing, despite being in the newspaper at this address. It is possible that the house was demolished or destroyed in some incident. However, the mystery of the headless man has vanished as well. There have not been any further reports of any headless man, at least from what this author could find. Was he a miner? A John? We will likely never know.

Many brothels were lost in the State Street fires, but there are reminders, like the Pioneer Club, with memories of the red-light district flicker. Walking down these streets, one may notice particular frills on the houses, appearing with intricate awnings. Giant bay windows may have been used to showcase the offerings of these girls. Most of these homes are occupied; perhaps the residents know their homes' pasts. Perhaps they have their own Mabel or Ethel as a roommate. This is the historical red-light district, where the past meets the present while looking for a good time.

Do you keep the light on?

7
CITY OF THE DEAD

CITY CEMETERY AND EVERGREEN CEMETERY

Before Leadville became an official city, the first community member was buried in the local grounds. Over time, Leadville's death rate increased, and the city realized it needed more land for interment. This led to the establishment of Evergreen Cemetery on the north end of town. Many of its original graves were moved to a new location, but some bodies may have been forgotten. However, the spirits will not let anyone forget.

During Queen Victoria's reign (known as the Victorian era), death became a fascination. When she lost her husband in 1861, the queen remained in a state of grief for the remainder of her life. After President Abraham Lincoln's assassination in 1895, his funeral became the first "celebration of death." Funeral practices became extraordinary, including a display of the body and a long mourning period. Thus, death became a show.

The Victorians kept to their traditions when it came to death. Wakes were held in a family member's living room before the bodies were transported to the cemetery. This was done to keep an eye on the person in case they woke up, as being buried alive was a real fear. Someone sat with the corpse at all hours; superstition dictated that the spirit might leave the body. The spirit fleeing was a valid concern. Mirrors were often covered to prevent the spirit from becoming attached to them and getting stuck. Windows in the house were shut to keep the spirit inside. As the body was taken out of the house, the feet went first to keep the spirit from "beckoning another family member to follow him or her to the grave," according to April Slaughter and Troy Taylor in their 2018 book *Disconnected from Death.*

The cost of burying a body depended on the various costs of the burial, accommodations and labor. An 1879 article in the *Leadville Daily/Evening Chronicle* remarked that a pauper grave in New York cost around twenty-five dollars, likely cheaper if a body was going into a grave with other bodies. In Leadville, a grave cost only few dollars, which was used to pay the gravedigger for a plot that was "all nice and dry for all to himself," according to the same article. Many of the dead were paupers, unable to pay the increasing funeral costs. The reporter for the newspaper noted that the burials were no questions asked—a person could bring a body to be buried without a death certificate, and "no one will take the time to investigate." The article continued that a "grave, stained box, and dead-wagon" cost twenty-five dollars for a top-notch burial in Leadville with high-class additions. Professional mourners could be paid to bemoan at the funeral for five to ten dollars if one wanted a grand display of wailing despair and wallowing sorrow. Death was nothing to cry at.

The Irish community took mourning to another level. Often, they celebrated by holding a wake, where the body was brought into the house. Family and friends would keep vigil over the deceased, telling stories over bottles of whiskey or stout. According to Roger Pretti, there was more than one time when a dead body was displaced from the coffin, propped up and offered a beverage in their name.

The first city cemetery was laid out at the end of Chestnut and Pine Streets, and it was as large as an acre. The first interment was that of Captain Sullivan Breece, a sixty-two-year-old miner from Philadelphia, on November 17, 1877. Vincent Kreig held many jobs in the cemetery as an undertaker/grave digger and sexton. A terrible record-keeper, he never documented the burials, leaving several unknowns. When he died the following February, all that information went with him to his spot in the ground at the city cemetery. Harry Talhurst, Kreig's predecessor, started documenting the graves in the spring of 1879, but many records were later lost or destroyed.

Among the first documented graves of the cemetery include that of the city's first marshal, George O'Connor, who died on April 23, 1878, after he was shot five times by a fellow officer at William Nye's Saloon.

The *Leadville Daily/Evening Chronicle* wrote up the "city of the dead." Thomas Whistler Anderson was a child who passed on November 26, 1877; someone wrote a poem for the marker:

Far upon the mountain side
We lay our darling, our little pride
Dear, yes dearer to us was he
Than earth and all its wealth could be.

As the city grew with the establishment of Leadville in early 1878, so did the death rates. People moved into the city with spreadable diseases, and one of the number one causes of death was pneumonia. Other deaths included those from excessive alcohol consumption, mining incidents and suicide. A visitor to the city remarked that he counted twenty deaths in the two days he was in Leadville. One woman had just moved to the area, acknowledging that numerous funeral processions had passed her residence. A druggist who had a shop near the undertaker counted the graves in January 1879, which totaled no more than one hundred.

This number continued to increase, as burials included those of individuals from within a ten-mile radius. In February 1879, 115 graves were counted at the cemetery. By May 12, 1879, the number of graves increased to 254, and it was noted that something needed to be done.

An article in the May 26, 1879 *Leadville Daily/Evening Chronicle* describes a reporter's observation of the cemetery's overgrowth and lack of luster. Marble stones and wood markers indicated scattered graves, and very few of the wood markers had been painted to look as if they were marbleized. Mounds of carbonated red clay were in piled heaps near where they had been dug from the fresh earth. The reporter noted, "There is nothing about the buryying [*sic*] place for the dead of Leadville to make a well man want to die."

The city council soon gathered to discuss moving the cemetery to a new location. Cities were often judged based on the upkeep of their burial grounds, and the city cemetery did not help with the appeal. A local man, Stevens, deeded his land to the city with one condition: the city must fence the land and keep it clear. A sexton would also need to be employed to maintain the land. This was too good of a deal, plus Stevens was portioning a section of Capitol Hill for government business, such as court and jail.

On November 8, 1879, papers were filed for the Evergreen Cemetery Association to maintain and manage the new resting place for Leadville residents. Before the end of the month, the cemetery was interring bodies; however, the first report of a burial was said to have occurred on October 18, 1879. By the end of the year, sixty burials had occurred.

The old city cemetery was set to be abandoned, with approximately seventy-three out of the hundreds of bodies moved to the newly established Evergreen Cemetery on the edge of the town. According to the 1982 Historical Research Cooperative of Leadville, the abandoned graves were crossed over when the railroads laid tracks in 1880. Several of the graves still had relatively fresh bodies, not yet fully decomposed. One could only imagine the pungent smell, which residents rightfully complained about. A reporter for the town's newspaper visited the old cemetery in September 1880, saying it was "deplorable" that the train ran over the old resting place. Some coffins were nearly at surface level, under just a "few inches of dirt." Other graves were buried under dirt and stone piles, and the reporter was concerned that those individuals may never be known again.

One spirit of a highway robber decided it had some unfinished business in 1887. The *Leadville Daily/Evening Chronicle* reported hauntings occurring at the old cemetery almost nightly (except for Sundays) at 9:00 p.m. The spirit rose from a grave that had not been moved to Evergreen Cemetery. Upon the spirit's grand entrance, it knocked over its wooden marker and demanded a passerby to give it either their money or their lives—which worked. When the locals had enough, they decided to ambush the ghost, which apparently rose an hour earlier and reportedly beat them up. The newspaper article continued, "The residents decided to become reconciled to the ghost and trouble him no further." Meanwhile, a drummer from a baking powder firm visited the town in December 1887. Upon hearing about the phantom, the man decided to check it out for himself. Unphased by the overdramatic ghost, he spoke directly to the ghastly bandit, recalling a story of feeding a bothersome bear some baking powder. The substance caused the bear to explode! Considering this tale, the ghost shifted uncomfortably, before replying that it would no longer bother the living: "If you came here with the intention of driving me away, you have succeeded in your purpose; adieu!" With that, it retreated into its grave. There was no further word of the ghostly robber harassing the living at the old cemetery again.

Meanwhile, Evergreen Cemetery was opened to new burials in 1879. Religious sects purchased lots to have their parishioners buried, and family plots were obtained to keep everyone together. Men worked long hours to ensure trees were maintained, debris was cleaned and leisurely paths and roads were laid for mourners to visit their loved ones. Compared to the 1-acre city cemetery, Evergreen opened with 147 acres, promising proper burials.

By the end of 1880, 767 burials were recorded, a testament to the size of the growing city. In 1881, Congress donated a parcel of land for the veterans to be used for the United Veteran's Hospital and cemetery; the hospital closed in 1886, and the land was returned to the cemetery association.

By 1892, burials were organized by the funeral director. His job was to be punctual, to prevent the mourners from seeing the behind-the-scenes processes and to relieve the stress of the bereaved. The director did everything, from connecting with the clergy, organizing a choir, sending telegrams and ensuring the horse and carriage were clean and groomed.

After the silver panic concluded, many became impoverished and unable to pay for a funeral. Plots cost approximately fifteen dollars, a week's worth of a miner's wages. Those who could not afford these costs were buried in designated *free* religious sectors without markers; an attempt was made to match the deceased with their preferred religion. More than 1,300 were buried in unmarked graves, including 100 stillborn babies. It is estimated that 80 percent of the unmarked graves were prepared for the Irish. The Leadville Irish Miners Memorial remembers the unknown Irish who were buried in the Catholic free sections.

By the end of the 1880s, the Catholic church had built its cemetery, St. Joseph Cemetery, and some of the Evergreen interments were moved to the new hallowed grounds. The cemetery can be found by driving west on McWethy Drive.

Today, twelve sections divide the Evergreen Cemetery; these sections include the burials of not only old Catholics but also Protestants; Hebrews (the Jewish section's name); and members of the Patriotic Order of Sons of America, Knights of Pythias, the Masonic and Eastern Star Association, the Benevolent Protective Order of the Elks, the Grand Army of the Republic, the Ancient Order of the Union Workmen and Odd Fellows. The cemetery is open to new burials if you want to lay eternally next to Leadville's finest residents.

Notable graves in the cemetery include those of John B. "Texas Jack" Omohundro, the partner of the Wild West showman Buffalo Bill Cody. Texas Jack was also a Civil War Confederate soldier. While performing in the show that showcased life in the West, he met his wife, Italian ballerina Giuseppina (or Josephine) Morlacchi. Sparks flew the moment their eyes locked. They were wed in 1873 and went on the road. In 1876, the pair broke off from the Wild West show to form their Texas Jack Combination Show. This show led them to Leadville, which they decided to call home. Sadly, after three months of living in the Cloud City, Texas Jack contracted pneumonia and died. After a glorious funeral at the Tabor Opera House, he was buried in Evergreen.

Overcome by grief, Giuseppina left for their old home in Massachusetts, never to perform again. Six years later, she lost her life to cancer and was laid to rest in Lowell, Massachusetts, across the country from her beloved. When Buffalo Bill visited Leadville almost thirty years later, he noticed the state of the wooden marker at his friend's grave. In 1908, he commissioned a new monument, which stands as a testament to the traveling showman.

In 1885, the Homestake Avalanche took the lives of ten miners in February, but they were not discovered until April. One man still possessed a letter dated February 22 that he had yet to mail. No one knew about the avalanche's damage until people noticed the miners had not been in town in some time. The bodies were brought back thanks to the efforts of one hundred volunteers on snowshoes. Chris Harvey's body was sent down the mountain to Central City for burial, and James Burns was brought back to California for interment. The other men, Horace and Josiah Matthews, Sylvester and Mortin Borden, Charles Richards, John Locke, Robert Campbell and Thomas Burt, were buried under a memorial in the Evergreen Cemetery. The six-foot-tall memorial with a mourning grief atop stands in remembrance of the tragic incident.

Near the Homestake memorial stands a pine tree that marks Mollie May's grave. According to a Leadville by Lamplight tour guide, Rhone, as Mollie lay dying, she had her girls promise her one thing. Sure, they said, they would do anything for Mollie. Mollie asked to be buried at Evergreen with only a single tree planted above her as a marker. While Mollie was brought in that expensive hearse to her final resting place, covered with countless flowers and followed by a long procession, none of the city's elite came to pay their respects.

Tom Dickson has two graves in the Evergreen Cemetery, one marked and another unmarked. There are unknown reasons for this, according to Roger Pretti. Could it be due to the notion that Dickson was a wanted man and was shot during an attempted burglary? He and a buddy had burst into a saloon when the proprietor shot him dead between the eyes. The buddy fled initially, only to return to ensure his "friend" was dead. Dead men could not tell tales. Legend says that Dickson was buried in the clothes he fell in, but which grave does he lie in?

In 1902, a young man entered the Pioneer Club at 11:00 a.m. The saloon was deserted; he asked for a match to light his pipe and went to the back of the club, where he promptly shot himself. Oscar Ellison was

Homestake Avalanche Memorial recognizes those lost in Evergreen Cemetery. *Author's collection.*

twenty-five years old and in love with a young lady named Nellie, who did not return his affection. In his suicide note, he begged to be taken to the coroner, not his home where his mother was alone. Inside his pocket was a twenty-dollar bill, he instructed as to pay the bill for his funeral. However, what had happened? He had just returned from Denver, where he had written letters to his parents and Nellie. The note to the young lady read, "This is the last." She cried, claiming she did not think he was serious when he expressed admiration. A package Oscar had shipped himself arrived that morning; it held new clothes and a ring Oscar had intended to give Nellie. Instead, Oscar was dead five hours later. Today, love scorned, he rests in the Evergreen Cemetery.

One notable person's grave may or may not be in the Evergreen Cemetery. *The Herald Democrat*'s visitors guide suggests that the wife of the Colorado Cannibal may be buried in Leadville. Flora Packer moved to Leadville, where she resided on East Chestnut Street, "without a scratch of a pen to identify her." Those who got to know her discovered that she had once been a mistress of Alferd Packer, the "man-eater," who was serving time for murder in the Canõn City penitentiary. In February 1874, Packer guided a group of men through the snowy mountains when they became stranded at Chief Ouray's camp. Ignoring the chief's warning about the weather, Packer and five men traveled on, where they became lost in the snow. After Packer stumbled out of the mountains alone two months later, an investigation ensued. The other men had died naturally when Packer and Shannon Bell survived via cannibalism. Packer insisted that he shot Bell in self-defense. After a lengthy legal process and Packer's resistance, he was sentenced to spend forty years in prison. Eventually, he was paroled and lived the rest of his days in Littleton, Colorado, where he reportedly became a vegetarian. Flora did not talk much about her past life but maintained constant interest during his trial. After she died in 1888, her friends rallied to provide her with a coffin for burial. There is no indication of where she may be buried in the cemetery.

This chapter would not be complete without tales of the occult or restless spirits that float around their final resting spots. Perhaps there is a state of unrest. Take, for example, the old Leadville City Cemetery at the intersection of Chestnut and Pine Streets. Railroads traveled over the desecrated graves, and other roads were paved over countless bodies; however, today, many of the unknown bodies lie under Lake County High School's football field. According to research by Roger Pretti, there are about one hundred bodies still underneath the field. Some have been murmuring that the spirits may have been to blame for poor games or practice sessions. The school has since developed a new field where the team plays—away from the old graveyard.

Stories have, for years, reflected supernatural claims in Evergreen Cemetery, such as witnessing unexplained blue lights emanating from the tops of the trees. However, science may describe this phenomenon as "foxfire," a bioluminescent glow emitted by certain fungi on dead limbs. Could it be explained? Or could it be the wispy, flowing apparition of Erona, the spirit of the deer woman, making her way through the cemetery?

Walking through the cemetery, you may see markers labeled "Hung." This was the grave of at least one of the five men who were hanged at the gallows. One man's grave tells a fascinating tale related to the dark arts. Si Meunich (or "Minich") was sentenced to be hanged for the murder of Samuel Baldwin. He also stole money from the dead man and committed a spending spree without hesitation. He claimed his innocence until he drew his last breath as he stood on the gallows near St. Joseph Cemetery. An estimated three to seven thousand were in attendance at his execution.

City Cemetery as it appears today. *Author's collection.*

Sheriff Lamping "revolted at the idea of hanging an innocent man" and was assured that the guilty man would have confessed without his attorney's objections. Si was buried in the back of the cemetery in a pauper's grave, alone in death. However, he would not remain alone.

Years after Si's death, it became apparent that the grave site was either sinking, or the dirt around it was going missing, as the coffin started poking through the earth at the bottom of the hole. Soon, rumors alleged that certain members of the community dabbled in the dark arts, such as witchery and necromancy, and were taking dirt from graves. In an 1898 article of *The Herald Democrat*, there was a report of an older woman from the east side of town who was known for her "hoodoo" or "black magick." Neighbors speculated that the woman hid in her kitchen, boiling up various spells made of animal parts, and when the woman learned of the neighbors' gossip, she sought revenge. One evening, the mysterious woman entered the cemetery to snag a pail full of dirt from Meunich's grave. Then, just before midnight, she went house to the house of those who'd done her wrong and "threw dirt against the door, muttering to herself some sort of incantations." The next day, the folks who lived there could not help but notice the piles of dirt that confirmed their strange neighbor's witchy behavior.

A neighborhood watch was put forth, as the woman had been to the cemetery with her dirt pail twice now. A woman from the "council of war" was familiar with old country superstitions and thought the incantation had come from an ancient rhyme:

Home and fireside naught will be save
When cursed thrice from murderer's grave
Dirt that covers a hangman's prey
Bringith mis'ry should it lay
By health, by home, by yard, by door
Thrown thrice in the midnight hour.

By the third night, the mystery woman was discouraged by the group waiting for her at the murderer's grave. The newspaper noted that she left, not by broom, but by hurriedly walking away—but not before she threw dirt at the women and uttered some incantation. While the newspaper did not identify the woman, this may have been Lizzie "Hoodoo" Brown. This woman lived on upper East Chestnut Street, where she turned to alcohol and worked in the red-light district. Wagging tongues around town said that she worked closely with the devil and had allegedly cursed local men in the area.

Accounts of using graveyard dirt for spell work have existed for centuries, with traces dating back to Greek and Medieval European cultures. The dirt from a criminal's grave was thought to have held supernatural powers, and people could use the dirt (even a pinch) from a grave to hex another. The dirt from a grave was also believed to be a method of spirit transmission and communication. Evil spirits could be warded off by graveyard dirt or dustings. Today, graveyard dirt is still ritually collected by practitioners for multiple reasons, such as protection, love or curses, showcasing its versatility.

At the beginning of Leadville's inception, the city cemetery started as a tiny one-acre plot of land that quickly became overgrown and needed expansion. As the city's population grew, its death rates increased, leading to the development of a larger cemetery across town. The states of rest may be why these spaces are known for their hauntings. None of the stories appear ill-willed (and Si's grave has not been messed with in some time), and perhaps the stories of these past residents only want to be heard.

Cemeteries are not to be feared. They are places of eternal rest, a soft voice on the breeze, each grave holding the story of a dreamer, the hopeful and the inspired, those who wanted a new life, a better life and some who never got the chance. Even those who made unfortunate and poor choices to seek glory had a story. Every marker and every monument holds the memory of a person who lived among the clouds. The forgotten and the nameless all have a story. Close your eyes, listen to the breeze and feel the wind on your skin. If you listen, the spirits of those who sleep here may tell you their stories. All you have to do is listen.

8
SPIRITUALISM IN CLOUD CITY

The Spiritualism movement was born on a chilly March day in 1848 in Hydesville, New York. Sisters Maggie, Leah and Kate Fox gave rise to communicating with spirits through the development of rapping, essentially knocking. While living with their parents in a one-room cottage, teenagers Maggie and Kate claimed the house was haunted. The girls asked questions about the spirit in the home, which were answered via an alphabet system. The parents seemed to have forgotten the date was March 31, the day before April Fool's Day. The sisters were sent to live with their older sister, Leah, in Rochester and demonstrated this skill with neighbors. Rumors took off and circulated. The public said this was fantastic, and they wanted more communication with the dead. Soon, the Fox sisters were conducting séance tours, and others were coming out of the woodwork, claiming they could also talk to the dead. Despite Maggie admitting that the entire act was a fraud in 1888, people were sensationalized by spirit communication. The Victorians were very much into the idea of communication after death. According to an article from *The Herald Democrat*, spiritualism encompassed "a calm reassurance of superior knowledge, assert the existence of spirit life, and the phantoms of the dead are in the habit of revealing themselves through human understanding" through mediums and other clairvoyants. This included the curiosity of the folks in Leadville, albeit some who did not fall for gimmicks. If it was not for so-called mediums and clairvoyants coming to town to peddle their tricks, other suspects' supernaturalistic abilities may have been seen by peers in the form of witchcraft.

One notable and controversial medium made the trek across the United States to the mountain town. Maud E. Lord (or Lord-Drake) was a popular psychic whose claim was her numerous meaningful readings, including two for Queen Victoria. In 1878, two years after visiting nearby Georgetown, she mysteriously disappeared while en route to Brocton via her home in Boston. Despite a cause of police involvement and alarm, she seemed to reappear without a known reason. She visited Leadville in 1881 for a few weeks and mesmerized the town. The *Leadville Democrat* wrote, "She walks in like beauty like the Night [*sic*] of starry [illegible] and cloudless nights." Among a group of twenty or so individuals, she started to open communication with loved ones and showed the location with a clapping of hands. The *Rocky Mountain News* was invited to a semiformal séance at a local hall. The reporter was directed to place his feet on top of hers to ensure there was no tomfoolery in her *tests* (the tests were said to be of evidential mediumship). Immediately, activity started occurring in the space, and the reporter felt the presence of a child sitting on his lap. Touching the reporter's face, the ghostly child murmured, "I want to see my momma." Another observer in the crowd apparently drew the attention of several spirits, and the woman became so upset that she begged the spirits not to harm her. Meanwhile, a grieving widow felt the kiss of her beloved husband; she became "excited and inclined to be hysterical, the spirit, whatever else it was, vanished."

It was stated that Maud had "converted" the people of Leadville, and in awe of her abilities, they presented her with a rare silver ingot.

By 1891, Maud boasted that she had contributed to naming California's Stanford University, expressing that the dead son of Leland Stanford and his wife, Jane, wished to have his name on the university. The bereaved parents scoffed, claiming they had had the name chosen six months before they met for a reading. By 1892, the Stanfords labeled Maud Lord as a "fraud who had no more to do with it than a child unborn." Never faltering, Maud continued her tours. She visited the nearby city of Aspen often, and in 1893, the papers declared, "Her manifestations are the most wonderful of any medium that has ever visited the city." Whether Maud was a legitimate speaker to the dead or pulling the wool, she made a mark on the silver mining city and surrounding mountain towns.

While some of these séances were held in parlor rooms of the town's higher-class buildings, there were larger shows that needed an equivalent space. The Tabor Opera House was built in 1879, when Horace Tabor decided that Leadville needed the fine entertainment the elite received out east. The red brick building was built in one hundred days to the amazement

The stage of the Tabor Opera House as it looks today. *Author's collection.*

of citizens, but it was not the most appealing yet to the public. On opening night, November 20, 1879, the seats did not sell out for the production of *The Serious Family*. Another show was happening down the street: a group of vigilantes staged a double hanging. Eventually, the shows, such as séances that could fill a house, gained interest over the gallows.

In 1882, J.B. and C.H. Miller filled the house with a standing-room-only crowd. Initially, J.B. informed the house that they did not consider their "powers to be supernatural," since there were many critics; the audience could decide for themselves. The men put on a spectacle show, whether they were tricks, slights of hand or conversations with the dead. After the show, C.H. invited a news reporter to the hotel for a reading the following day. However, when the reporter called the hotel to check in, he was informed that the psychic duo checked out in the early morning. The plan to leave early was decided the day prior, said the hotel staff, so why the invite? The reporter was bemused, "This contradiction certainly might impress an unbeliever that there was fraud somewhere."

A year later, another show was put on by Annie, or Anna, Eva Fay down on Fifth Street at the Zoo Theatre. The *Daily Herald* stated, in a "scientific séance, the only woman in the world with the endorsement of the members of the Royal Scientific Society of London," she claimed to be able to materialize faces and flowers, tip tables and communicate with spirits. The great Harry Houdini, who was loudly skeptical of Spiritualism, claimed that she once told him that she tricked society by hiding things under her skirt. Whether she was a fraud or not, Annie knew how to wow the audience.

Speaking of Houdini, there is speculation that he performed at the Tabor Opera House, and the trapdoor on the stage was measured to his specifications. The mysterious thing is that there is no factual evidence that he ever stepped foot into Leadville.

More rumors circulate about the opera house being haunted, but no recorded evidence of this exists. There are only whisperings, no written details. Visit Leadville and take a tour. Listen to the past to find if it is haunted or not.

While spiritualism was hot, there was controversy over whether a medium was legitimate. There were at least two who were impressive to the public. A young man named Chas B. Brockway was said to always be able to fill a room and have everyone in attendance fully confident in his abilities. He

The interior of the Tabor Opera House as it appeared in 1879. *Photo by Alfred Brisbois.*

amazed a crowd at city hall and Weston Opera House (formerly the Tabor) when answered questions hidden away in sealed envelopes, which were also tucked away from his eye. His readings were described as "so clean and perfect that people admire them, although they cannot understand them."

When Mrs. Dr. Calder performed a séance at city hall, she identified people in the audience and their deceased loved ones—she was a stranger to Leadville, so it was unknown how she might have known that information unless she was psychic. Later, she performed at 140 West Seventh Street; the *News Reporter* boasted that her readings were "positive demonstrations of accurate and genuine work."

The Occult Society of Leadville was formed around this time as a part of the National Spiritualist Association (NSA). This group was formed in Chicago in 1893 and focused on combating fraudulent mediums in the community and helping avoid legal ramifications. *The Herald Democrat* described the demographics, which included "bright men and women who have devoted much of their leisure time to ferreting...Voodooism, witchcraft, necromancy, the existence of astral bodies, and the existence of the spirits of the departed."

George Schafer, a one-time bidding president of the society, moved into a cottage at the junction of Tenth and Hazel Streets, aware that it might be haunted. The cellar was said to have trapped souls, and Schafer wanted to get to the bottom of it. The group investigated reported supernatural phenomena and happily held tests for incoming psychics and mediums to assess abilities. One of the society members was put under hypnosis, and an otherworldly being spoke through her. The supposed spirit informed the group that under the cellar floor, they would find the bones of a child. Well, some men dug the next day...and found nothing. A news reporter said some community members chalked it up to the fact that, sometimes, transmissions can be wrong, and people should be quiet about it.

Spiritualists were either loved or despised. Some brought entertainment and/or comfort from the spirit world, and some took advantage of the bereaved. The Victorian era embraced this unique ability, but it soon lost its charm. The age of Spiritualism had dwindled by the end of the 1940s and melted into the communities of paranormal research and the psychical/metaphysical fields we see today.

WITCHES OF LEADVILLE

Some individuals of Leadville with eccentric characteristics or abilities were not as sweetly labeled as psychics or mediums. The word *witch* came to mind when women were suspected of ill-doings that caused pain and misfortune. Were these misunderstood women, like the so-called *old woman* who came down from the nearby hills and begged from any passersby? The unnamed elderly woman was accompanied by fellow vagrants who may have been traveling thieves. Her appearance was horrid, as she was described as having a withered face, and she spoke poor English. Her appearance frightened many women and children who looked at her. How did people know she was a witch? A neighboring farmer said so.

The *Leadville Daily/Evening Chronicle* speculated, "During the night, she takes a journey through the air to join her companions in some witch dance in a lonely place in the mountains." After the witch cured an ailing baby in Twin Lakes, the mother, Mrs. Jenkins, became ill and asked to also be cured. The old woman neither accepted nor declined. Instead, she left for three days, and upon her return, she claimed that an evil-possessed cow had afflicted Mrs. Jenkins. What becomes even stranger is that the witch said there were thirty-three feather-shaped witch balls under Mrs. Jenkins's bed that needed to be burned. (Yes, the balls were oddly found, as described.) Once this occurred, the witch said the cow would die, and Mrs. Jenkins would be completely healed. Sure enough, after these steps were completed, the cow died, and the woman's health improved. At night while she slept, Mrs. Jenkins was instructed to wear something that appeared to be made of an animal's bladder and created quite the unpleasant smell. The witch claimed this would dispel others evil entities from causing further trouble. Citizens of Leadville were unsure if the old woman was an actual witch, a beggar or some "good fairy." Just as she arrived, the old woman mysteriously disappeared soon after this incident and did not appear to return to the Cloud City.

In 1899, a woman was brought to the court, accused of witchcraft. Catherine Rothenberg moved to Leadville within the year with her husband and child. The *Star Tribune* indicated in an article that her appearance was quite noticeable, as she was described as an exotic, "beautiful Jewess," with the control of a "dead and Arabian sage as a geni." With this control, she could assist her neighbors with their questions. Not all saw her power as something good. Some community members said they saw her eyes roll and shoot fire during midnight walks in the cemetery. Someone spouted the rumor that Catherine was gathering dirt from the criminal Si Meunich's grave so that she could use it to inflict illness on folks who had done her wrong. One family alleged that they contracted measles from a bit of the murderer's grave dirt she sprinkled in their water. Out of a dozen witnesses, one Martin Roberts had drawn the accused witch's blood. Despite his skepticism, the man had heard of her unique gift and later testified that he initially sought her advice over a mining plan. Amazed, he bet the beautiful woman $100 that she could not give him additional information on a side project. Of course, she provided him with detailed context. Blown away, he went home to his wife to tell her all about this incredible conversation.

Mrs. Roberts dismissed the essence of mysticism, confronting the so-called witch about the fraud. An upset Catherine made a threat of illness to the Roberts family, including insanity and the disabling of their child. "You shall feel the power you take such pains to scorn." That night, Martin's head started to madly hurt, which caused the couple to fear that the threat was real. He testified that he was under a spell but remembered that Catherine admitted once during a friendly chat that the only counter-curse was to cause her mouth to bleed. This was when Roberts broke into Catherine's house to attack the accused witch. "My power is gone!" Police arrested the attacker after he arrived home, and he freely expressed why she had it coming.

After everything was taken into account, Martin's charge was dismissed, albeit he had to pay a thirty-dollar charge for "blood-letting." His head malady was gone; physicians had no logical reason for this occurrence. Roberts told a newspaper reporter that "the world can laugh...but I know that for months I was helpless under the hypnotic influence of the she devil." Catherine Rothenberg denied any witchery behaviors, although she may have been considered a spiritual medium or clairvoyant. She eventually left Leadville with her family and went to Denver. Catherine died in 1923 and was buried in Mount Nebo Memorial Park in Aurora, Colorado.

Then there was Elizabeth "Lizzie" Brown, who traveled to Leadville from Buena Vista. According to historian Roger Pretti, Lizzie's early years were unknown, but she found her way up to Buena Vista around 1879, where she met her common-law husband, "Hoodoo" Brown. The two took up with pickpocketing, and Hoodoo had a gambling habit. Hoodoo and his opponent "Curley" Frank took to dueling outside during one gruesome game in 1880. Neither won, as both were fatally shot by the other. Hoodoo perished almost immediately, while Curley expired a few hours later. Despite being well-known opponents, the dead men were buried in one grave.

The original courthouse as it appeared circa 1882–90. *Photo by William Henry Jackson.*

Lizzie moved quickly to Leadville, where she worked in the red-light district to earn a living. Some newspaper accounts identify her by her husband's moniker, "Hoodoo," as she was noted for her quarrels with other girls or troubles with the law.

By 1885, gossip around town muttered that Lizzie conspired with the devil and practiced nefarious acts. In the same year, a man named M.J. McConnell was charged with assault after responding to Lizzie's dare to hit her. The judge gave him several hours to get out of town. M.J. was surprised to learn that the same woman may have cursed Amos Young. As Amos left for the nearby town of Aspen, he contracted a fever and broke his leg. His brother Achilles hauled him over the mountain range. They sought help from an Aspen-based medium, who proclaimed that first a Leadville-Aspen connection had to be made to counter the curse. Achilles's fiancée's blood was injected into his arm to create a needed bond as he went on to Leadville without her. M.J. accompanied him back to Cloud City, as he was being paid to do the complicated task of killing the witch's cat by chopping it in two. The medium needed to know immediately when this occurred. A unique bracelet was given to the fiancée, and she was directed to wear it under the full moon; when it pinched her wrist, the medium knew it was time. Once the young bride-to-be cried out, Amos opened the door in Aspen. At the same time, the cat's dissected tail-end was said to have flown through the open doorway, which the psychic kicked into the lit fire of the stove. Amos was cured!

The following year, another man claimed to be under the influence of a spell. James Palmer started experiencing wild hallucinations after going after "Rustler" Blobson, who reportedly wanted to harm him. He found himself behind bars as well—and possibly behind a curse. The confused man was informed that Blobson and another named "Tinhorn" Epps had made a deal with Lizzie to curse James. Was Lizzie behind these strange anomalies?

Strange occurrences seemed to follow Lizzie. On one fateful day in 1888, the marshal of nearby Breckenridge visited Leadville. Police were alerted to Lizzie's house by Ellen Smith, who asked officials to come quickly; a man was dead at her house on State Street. Lizzie, Ellen and another shady character named "Banjo" Bob were arrested for the death of William H. Watson. All three claimed to have had nothing to do with the suspected morphine poisoning. Per testimony, morphine had been procured for a good time and set into some oyster soup or beer. Ellen proclaimed that Lizzie was always getting her into trouble. However, Ellen had no problem getting into trouble for herself. As there was no convincing evidence that this was a case of murder, the court dismissed the charges. Was this an accidental death or a well-covered murder?

Death came for Lizzie "Hoodoo" Brown in 1901, and she was buried in an unmarked grave in the Catholic St. Joseph's Cemetery down the road from Evergreen Cemetery. Interestingly, how could a rumored witch be allowed burial in hallowed ground?

While communication with the dead may have been a controversial topic, Spiritualism was a big fad during the Victorian era in Leadville. Public spaces sold out for society to hear the *tests* of a so-called medium or clairvoyant to read the unknown. Connecting with loved ones, reading minds or creating kinetic movements either wowed the public or caused some to denounce their abilities. Then some other individuals dabbled in the dark arts—or so rumor says. Leadville had both, and none of them exist today. Or do they?

9
Law and Order of Leadville

From the beginning of Leadville's development, there was a need for structure and order, as dreamers and seekers flowed in droves to town. Not everyone had good intentions, as some deviants chose a life of crime to get what they wanted. Some found themselves without other means to bring in income and resorted to the means necessary to survive. Famous ruffians made their way through the streets of Leadville, such as conman Jefferson Randolph "Soapy" Smith. Smith manipulated folks by selling soap to them and claiming that if they bought the soap, they might win prize money. In front of a crowd, a customer unwrapped their new bar to find a celebratory $100 bill. This excitement enticed others to buy bars to try their luck impulsively. Of course, this was a whole set-up, as no bar of soap held the real winnings except for the one that was part of the trick.

It was a wild time in the Wild West. Marshals patrolled the streets, and criminals tried to elude capture. When they were not so lucky, the accused were hauled off to the city jail to have their day in court. Not everyone left the streets, and not everyone left the jail; some stayed in spirit. Let us prowl the streets of historic Leadville.

As Leadville became an established community, an election was held on February 12, 1878. Horace Tabor was appointed mayor, C.E. Anderson was appointed clerk and recorder, T.J. Campbell was appointed as judge, A.K. Updegraff was appointed as attorney and T.H. Harrison was appointed as town marshal. By April 1878, Harrison had resigned, and Mayor Tabor had appointed George O'Connor to the position. O'Connor was

The police force of Leadville, circa 1878–79. *Photo via Denver Public Library.*

murdered a month into the job while confronting one of his junior officers, James "Texas" Bloodsworth. The latter liked to frequent bar halls, which O'Connor disagreed with. On the night of the incident, O'Connor denied the accusation of calling Bloodsworth a coward. Attempts to de-escalate the situation failed, and O'Connor was shot five times before he stole the best horse in Leadville and ran out of town. So far, the position of town marshal was proving to be a challenging one.

Martin "Mart" Duggan was appointed the third marshal due to his burliness and no-nonsense behavior regarding lawbreakers. He had come to Leadville with nothing but his name, wandering the mines before taking on the role of the law. It was pretty clear that lawbreakers behaved themselves when Marshal Duggan monitored the streets, as crime increased when he left the force. P.A. Kelly succeeded Duggan, but Mart returned to serve another stint as marshal from 1879 to 1880, as Kelly could not brave the job. In November 1880, Duggan encountered Louis Lamb on Fifth Street outside one of the brothels. While transporting a sleigh to Winnie Purdy's house, Lamb was struck. Words were shouted, and pistols were drawn. Lamb never had a chance before the bullet hit its mark. Mart Duggan went straight to the police and was acquitted of any murder charges on the claim of self-defense. Mrs. Mindy Lamb, the widow, declared vengeance for her husband's death, spitting out that she would dance on Duggan's grave. Mollie May saw the whole thing transpire, and she came out to console the upset woman, claiming she knew Duggan was guilty of the crime. From then on, the two women were quick friends, something not common among the red-light district ladies. Mrs. Lamb attended Mollie's funeral.

One night in April 1888, a shot rang out in the dark outside a notorious gambling hall on Harrison Avenue, known as the Texas House. An unknown assailant had shot Mart Duggan. The shooter was initially said to be Bailey Youngson, but Duggan rescinded his accusation. The following day, the ground where Duggan had fallen was stained. A woman came out of the crowd of onlookers. "With the air of a priestess performing a rite, she began a solemn waltz on the darkened boards. It was Mrs. Lamb," wrote *The Herald Democrat*.

A man did not want to be caught alone on State and East Chestnut Streets. Men might drink too much, pass out and find themselves robbed after waking up. They wanted to avoid hearing the words "Hold up your hands!" shouted by a footpad hoping to make a quick buck. Most men carried a pistol as a form of protection. Many illicit behaviors were overlooked to avoid trouble, such as gambling and sex work. One visitor wrote home about the violence, expressing that one may not know who is next to die. Policing the area did little to stop the crime, due to the veracity of trouble. Fires occurred often, keeping the town's hose and ladder companies busy. One visitor noted that "if one didn't start, someone started it just to see the action." In the late summer of 1879, eight men were deputized by the sheriff as part of the Merchants' Protective Patrol. Like a neighborhood watch of today, these men reported anything suspicious to alert the uniformed officers.

Sometimes, the citizens took the punishment into their own hands.

On November 20, 1879, the Tabor Opera House opened its doors to the public for the first time. Not all the tickets sold out, as there was another show. Patrick Stewart and Edward Frodsham were being held in the city jail on suspicion of murder and lot jumping. Stewart and a colleague had attempted the robbery of a barber, Carl (also reported as Charlie) Bockhaus, who did not want to comply and shot Stewart's partner. Frodsham had been trying to steal Capitol Hill real estate lots. A vigilant crowd gathered outside the jail that November night to seek justice. Fifteen men were said to have entered the jail and seized the two men to hang them outside. Frodsham was said to have been afraid, and he fought for his life.

A note was attached to Frodsham's dead back as a notice to all criminals: "This is our commencement, and this shall be your fates. We mean business, and let this be your last warning....Vigilantes Committee. We are 700 strong." It is unknown who was among these men who quickly busted out the two accused to take their last steps on Earth.

Frodsham's ghost still has unfinished business; some believe his spirit still vies over lots to steal.

The old jail was not a pleasant place to be. It saw the likes of men, women, drunks, criminals, sex workers, etc. The cells were made of metal plates within the same materialistic cage. Cell 8 was always empty. Multiple inmates claimed it was haunted, and no one stood a chance of being housed within its walls. Allegedly, one inmate took his own life by suffocation, and while his body left the cell, his spirit stayed behind. Numerous times, inmates screamed to be let out of cell 8, claiming a "corpse with a blue mark around its neck had crawled into bed with them." Initially, guards were nonbelievers, but after several complaints—including one from a brutal bully who bargained, "String me up and whip me!"—the possibility of a haunting seemed likely.

The original courthouse and adjoining jail were demolished in the 1940s and rebuilt in the same spot. The jail still stands with its original bars and hauntings. In the early 2000s, complaints of cold gusts of air, television problems and moving objects came from the trustee's cell block without a valid reason. A brave soul decided to set out a tape recorder to try to

A look down Harrison Avenue around 1880–85; the original courthouse can be seen on the right. *Photo by William Henry Jackson.*

capture any phenomena. Paranormal investigators use this technique to capture electronic voice phenomena (also known as EVPs) to capture voices that might generally not be heard audibly—voices that might be considered spiritual in origin. The words "higher" and "bless me" were audible in the playback, along with questionable noises that sounded like they came from a male source. When a lieutenant reviewed the potential evidence, he said, as a religious man, "If that were me back there [referring to the trustee's cells away from the general population], I'd never go back there again." The trustees were specific inmates who worked in trusted jobs in the courthouse and jail. The spirit had given gifts to the trustees, such as granola bars and crosses, especially when a nylon cord cross was discovered hanging from a cell doorway. Who was this spirit, and were they trying to seek salvation?

Might this be Old Hank, whose spirit was floating around the jail in 1881? An inmate named Blake was spending his time in the jail cell when he heard Hank banging. Hank informed him that he was in "purgatory and asked Blake and the other boys in the jail to pray for him" so he could have penance and freedom. A news reporter later asked Blake if this was a spirit, not another inmate making noise. Blake was adamant it was the ghost, as did at least two other inmates.

The grave site of Merrick Rosengrantz. *Author's collection.*

Blake was also curious if the spirit was connected to the recent hangings of two convicted murderers only thirteen days prior. The gallows stood outside town, waiting to send the accused off this earth. The largest execution must have been that of Merrick Rosengrants (or Rosengrantz) and Francis Gilbert, who were legally hanged on double gallows on July 29, 1881. Both were accused of murder at Tennessee Park, several miles from the city. Rosengrants had been rifling through John Langmeyer's belongings the year prior when the victim confronted him. Rosengrants answered with his pistol, and the man died three days later. Gilbert killed James McCallum over money in 1880, claiming self-defense.

On the day of the men's hangings, the news reported they slept well, groomed themselves and wore new suits. Rosengrants tearfully proclaimed his innocence at the scaffold, while Gilbert stated, "I have made all the statements I wish to the reporters. That is all." Depending on the source, there were an estimated seven to ten thousand witnesses (men, women and children) to observe the deaths of these criminals. After the autopsy and burial at Evergreen Cemetery on the same day, the *Rocky Mountain News* noted, "The city is extremely quiet."

Cycling back to the spirit in jail, the question was: Who was Hank? Old Hank's spirit told Blake that Gilbert greeted him upon his death, as if he had died within the previous two weeks. Was he related to one of the recently condemned? Could he have been one of the men who died by suicide behind the steel bars? Other jail deaths were the results of overdoses, whether intentional or accidental. Perhaps one of these was his.

By 1884, a State Street woman by the name of Minnie was arrested due to her intoxication and carted off to the city jail. It was said she sobered up and, in despair of the life she was living, decided to end her life. Somehow, she obtained a bottle of poison, which she used to end her life. It was too late when someone walked by, as "the poor waif on life's troubled sea gave up the ghost in the cell," reflected a reporter of *The Herald Document.* Rumors of her death circulated, and inmates were wary of the cell Minnie in which died. The female inmates claimed that Minnie's ghost appeared to them, dressed in white, which terrified them. "It looked so sad," one inmate said of the apparition of Minnie. When the guard investigated, nothing was there, and they blamed shadows for the excitement.

The spirit of Si Meunich made its way around Leadville, as mentioned in other chapters. In 1886, he booked himself into the city jail before his body was laid in the paupers' field. According to *The Herald Democrat*, Mrs. Floody had just arrived at the jail for "creating a tempest" and shrieked when she saw the apparition of the dead man. Her new friend and cellmate, Ellen Smith, mourned the passing of the reportedly innocent man who died at the gallows for the murder of Sam Baldwin. His body was still being held at the local undertakers, awaiting burial planning. The bereaved woman shushed her friend and told her to not scare the spirit away, but Ellen could not see the spirit herself. It is unknown what the dead man wanted and why only one woman could see his apparition.

An 1897 account of a spirit at 118 West Fifth Street may also contribute to the hauntings of the jail. Once a brothel, the house is long gone now; a parking lot for government buildings occupies the space today. *The Herald Democrat* reported that the abandoned house once had a life of crime, murder and suicide. A young woman had gone missing, while a musician died from suspected poison, though an evaluation proved nothing. One night, George Sylvester got the scare of a lifetime as he walked home at midnight. As he passed 118 West Fifth Street, a light caught his eye from the desolate building that was once Winnie Purdy's ladies' boardinghouse. "The phantom, or whatever it was, raised its hands, and then came a most unearthly cry," wrote *The Herald Democrat.* Police had been called to check out strange activities at this house, but no living person was ever found upon inspection. Where did the spirit go? Was it one of the lives lost in the once-busy bordello? Could the spirit have made its residence in one of the government buildings?

Walking through the streets of Leadville, you might not realize how much occurred in the early years. From criminal depravity, many spots may have been the scene of someone's lost life. Many deaths, whether incidental or accidental, occurred on the streets and around the structures. Several buildings, like the Delaware Hotel, home of two separate murders, are still open for business. While many of the old buildings were demolished or destroyed in fires, could the energy of those spirits remain in the land they once knew as home? The West was wild in Leadville; although now, the dust has settled, and it is a quaint mountain town. Squint down Harrison Avenue for a moment. Against the clapboard buildings, you may see the horses tied to hitching posts along the dusty road. Quiet yourself. You may believe you can hear shouting, gunfire or music. Perhaps you will experience the auditory remnants of a town's past. Everyone came here for a reason—the hopes and dreams still linger. The energy of Leadville and its history remains strong. Visit and see for yourself.

BIBLIOGRAPHY

Altoona Tribune. "Leadville's Witch Trial." July 25, 1899.

Anthony, Susan B. "Susan B. Anthony Papers: Daybook and Diaries, 1877–1906." Manuscript/mixed material. Library of Congress.

The Aspen Times. "Round about Town." July 26, 1893.

"Baby Doe Wept on Tabor's Bier." *The Rocky Mountain News Daily* 76, no. 69 (March 10, 1935): 1.

Blair, Edward. *Leadville: Colorado's Magic City*. WestWinds Press, 1980.

The Carbonate Chronicle. "A Dance with Death." November 24, 1883.

———. "Dead!" September 11, 1880

———. "A Haunted House." June 16, 1883.

———. "A Stroll Through Leadville's Burying Grounds." September 4, 1880.

Churchhill, E. Richard. "Gallagher's Ghost." *The Daily Sentinel*, May 12, 1974.

"City of the Dead." *The Leadville Daily/Evening Chronicle* 1, no. 100 (May 26, 1879): 1.

The Daily Sentinel. "Coroner's Jury Writes Final Chapter in Leadville Case." April 19, 1949.

———. "Leadville Night Officer and Man He Tries to Arrest Shot to Death." April 8, 1949.

"The Death Rate." *The Leadville Daily/Evening Chronicle* 1, no. 12 (February 12, 1879): 1.

Ellman, Richard. *Oscar Wilde*. Vintage Books, 1987.

Explore Colorado. "Explore Colorado Haunted Leadville." YouTube. July 12, 2018. https://www.youtube.com/watch?v=qyOLOF79G3Y.

"A Ghost in the New Discovery Mine." *The Leadville Daily/Evening Chronicle* 1, no. 103 (May 28, 1879): 3.

Graff, Marshall Contant. "A History of Leadville." Master's thesis, University of Wisconsin, 1920.

Grim, Bekah. "A Brief History of Leadville." City of Federal Heights. https://www.fedheights.org/index.asp?SEC=%7BEFF67088-A3D7-4BA0-A840-A55F47A547F2%7D.

The Herald Democrat. "Ancient Beldame's Horrid Revenge." September 16, 1898.

———. "Banish 'Spook' from Its Haunts." April 11, 1907.

———. "Catching Ghosts." August 26, 1900.

———. "A Field of Psychical Research." February 22, 1897.

———. "Funeral Notes." January 11, 1888.

———. "A Ghost for a Guest." February 13, 1886

———. "Ghost in the City Jail." November 8, 1884.

———. "Haunted House Strange Lights." April 18, 1907.

———. "Haunted House Tenants Move." April 5, 1907.

———. "Hoodoo Brown." February 26, 1901.

———. "Lie on the Felon's Lip." February 6, 1886.

———. "Light and Shadows of Early Leadville." January 1, 1910.

———. "Over the Dark River." July 26, 1892.

———. "A Shade of Si Minnick in Demand.", July 8, 1899.

———. "Something about Ghosts." September 18, 1892.

———. "Spooks in Strawberry Gulch." April 6, 1886.

"He Saw a Ghost." *The News Reporter* 4, no. 282 (September 20, 1899): 1.

Historical Research Cooperative. "Original Leadville Cemetery. November 1877–November 1879." 1982. Lake County Public Library.

"History." Tabor Opera House. https://taboroperahouse.org/history.

"How Leadville Was Named." *The Leadville Daily/Evening Chronicle* 1, no. 86 (May 9, 1879): 1.

Johnston, Theresa. "Mrs. Stanford and the Netherworld." *Stanford Magazine*, May/June 2000.

Leadville and Twin Lake History Guide. O'Rourke Media Group/The Herald Democrat, 2024.

Leadville Daily Herald. Advertisement. December 23, 1883, 11.

———. "Death's Harvest." November 10, 1880.

———. "Sunday's Seance." June 20, 1882.

Leadville Democrat. "Maud E. Lord." June 23, 1881.

Leadville Evening Chronicle. "Decrees of Death." April 13, 1887, 4.

———. "Positive Facts." July 20, 1887, 4.

———. "Vanquishing the Ghost." December 21, 1887, 4.
———. "Witch of the Hills." July 29, 1890, 4.
"Leadville Sees but Little of Romance in Baby Doe." *The Rocky Mountain News Daily* 76, no. 70 (March 11, 1935): 5.
"Leadville's Redlight District Closed." *The Glenwood Post* 25, no. 5 (October 9, 1915): 6.
"Leadville Strike of 1896–97." *Colorado Encyclopedia*. https://coloradoencyclopedia.org/article/leadville-strike-1896-97.
"The Legendary Silver Dollar Saloon." Atlas Obscura. https://www.atlasobscura.com/places/the-legendary-silver-dollar-saloon.
"Local Law Makers." *The Leadville Daily/Evening Chronicle* 1, no. 23 (May 17, 1879): 1.
MacKell Collins, Jan. *Brothels, Bordellos, and Bad Girls: Prostitution in Colorado*. University of New Mexico Press, 2004.
———. *Good Time Girls of Colorado*. Twodot, 2019.
Manly, Nancy. "Evergreen Cemetery." *Mountain Diggings* 1, no. 7 (n.d.): 13–21. Lake County Public Library.
———. "Leadville City Cemetery." *Mountain Diggings* no. 15 (n.d.): 16–22. Lake County Public Library.
Martinek, Marcia. "Ghostly Tales Abound in This Old Mining Town." *The Herald Democrat*, October 25, 2017.
"A Modern Hero." *The News Reporter* 4, no. 179 (May 19, 1899): 1.
"Murdered His Wife." *The Rocky Mountain News Daily* 31 (November 5, 1889): 1.
"Old Hank's Ghost." *Leadville Weekly Herald* 2, no. 41 (August 13, 1881): 1.
"Over the Line." *The Rocky Mountain News Daily* 22 (July 30, 1881): 1.
Peterson, Roger. "Haunted Holes." *Vail Daily*, September 28, 2003.
———. "Jail Ghost Linked to 1884 Haunting." *Vail Daily*, July 8, 2004.
———. "Lake County Jail Oozes with Oddness." *Vail Daily*, June 2, 2004.
Pretti, Roger. "Ghosts of the Delaware Hotel Handout, Provided at the Hotel."
———. *Mining, Mayhem, and Other Carbonate Excitements. (Tales From a Silver Camp Named Leadville)*. Vail Daily, 2003.
"Public Séance Tonight." *The News Reporter* 4, no. 199 (June 12, 1899): 1.
Rudolph, Katie. "Newspaper Reports of a Leadville Haunting, 1907." October 13, 2020. Denver Public Library Special Collections and Archives.
"Silver Dollar Tabor Is Buried with No Family Present." *The Rocky Mountain News Daily* 66, no. 266 (September 23, 1925): 1.
"Spirit Land." *The Rocky Mountain News Daily* 22 (June 7, 1881): 4.
Sprague, Marshall. *Colorado: A History.* W.W. Norton & Company, 1984.

Star Tribune. "A Colorado Court Convicts a Woman of Being a Witch." December 3, 1899.

Taylor, Troy, and April Slaughter. *Disconnected From Death*. American Hauntings Ink, 2018.

Temple, Judy Nolte. *Baby Doe Tabor: The Madwoman in the Cabin*. University of Oklahoma Press, 2007.

Turner, Rosanna. "Exploring Historic Eagle County." *Vail Daily*, November 11, 2014.

Wilde, Oscar. *The Writings of Oscar Wilde*. Keller-Famer Co., 1907.

About the Author

As a native of Colorado, Erin Taylor is a passionate explorer of the unknown with a flair for storytelling and a keen understanding of the human psyche. With the release of her sixth book, *Haunted Leadville*, Erin continues to cement her reputation as a prolific author in the paranormal realm. Her previous works, including *Strange Colorado: Volume 2* (2024), *Unfinished Business #2* (2024), *Unfinished Business* (2023), *Strange Colorado: Volume 1* (2023) and *Sleeping Among Spirits* (2022), all self-published and available on Amazon, showcase her unique voice, engaging style and her great sense of humor. But her contributions don't stop at books; Erin is also a beloved regular contributor to *The Morbid Curious*, a publication by American Hauntings, and her insights have graced the pages of *Ghosted Magazine*, *American Paranormal Magazine* and *Haunted Magazine*.

Follow her on Facebook: @ETaylor.Author
And Instagram: @erintaylor_author